T0209960

# TRACER

Frederick Barthelme

COUNTERPOINT

Copyright © 1985 Frederick Barthelme

First Counterpoint paperback edition 2001

All rights reserved under international and Pan-American Copyright Conven-
tions. No part of this book may be used or reproduced in any matter whatso-
ever without written permission from the Publisher, except in the case of brief
quotations embodied in critical articles and reviews.

This book is a work of fiction. Names, characters, places, and incidents either
are products of the author's imagination or are used fictitiously. Any resem-
blance to actual events or persons, living or dead, is entirely coincidental.

Library of Congress Cataloging-in-Publication Data
Barthelme, Frederick, 1943-
    Tracer / Frederick Barthelme.—1st Counterpoint pbk. ed.
        p.   cm.
    ISBN 1-58243-129-9
    1. Triangles (Interpersonal relations)—Fiction.    2. Divorce—Fiction.
3. Florida—Fiction.    4. Sisters—Fiction.    I. Title.

PS3552.A763 T7 2001
813'.54—dc21                                                  00-065950

ISBN: 978-1-58243-129-1

COUNTERPOINT
2560 Ninth Street Suite 318
Berkeley, CA 94710

Printed in the United States of America

FOR RIE

I CHANGED AIRPLANES at Tampa, nodded when the flight attendant, a guy with stiff hair and freckles, told me the DC-3 was the safest thing in the air, and took a seat in the back.

I was getting away from my divorce, flying to Fort Myers to see my wife's sister, who operated a motel-condo on the Gulf near there. The divorce wasn't final, but I had agreed to give Alex whatever she wanted. People told me this was a bad idea, typical of first-time divorcees, but I hoped I'd feel better being generous. Also, I didn't want towels suddenly reminding me of her a year from now. Outside, the coast was shaped like a portrait silhouette. I spent the forty-minute trip watching the scenery and thinking of Alex, and occasionally wondering about the window, which looked as if somebody had been skating on it.

At the baggage claim a guy in a blue suit cupped his hand on my shoulder and asked if my name was Martin. I said it was, and then he started squeezing and unsqueezing. "Well, hi," he said. "I'm P. Rob Turner. Dominica sent me."

I said, "Hi," and looked around. "Is she here?"

"Nope," he said. "Couldn't catch you, couldn't work you into the schedule." He got my shoulder again and pointed me out the sliding-glass doors. "We're up here." He pointed toward a cream-colored Mercedes in the parking lot. "I'm a pal of hers. We've known each other for years. She's waiting for a real estate guy. Looking forward to your visit, though. I know that."

When we got moving he told me he'd been with Procter & Gamble but quit and moved to SeaSide —Dominica's motel—when he got his Pancake House. He'd waited a long time for his Pancake House, he told me. Then he talked about alligators, how he hoped we'd see one on the way. "I know where to go to see some," he said. "But I like it better when they just pop up, know what I mean? Out of nowhere."

We drove for forty minutes to a town called Lullaby that had one street that was about half-and-half abandoned and not-quite-abandoned buildings—a drug store, a gas station with yellow globes on the pumps—then we ran into a beach and the road swerved along the water. In a couple of minutes things opened up and that was it— buildings on one side of the road, Gulf on the other. On the beach side there were a couple of jetties and a restaurant with a neon bird for a sign.

Dominica was in the parking lot waiting for us. She had a burr haircut. She looked like somebody in boot camp, except up close she had perfect cheekbones, yellow specks in her irises, and this walking-dead makeup. She was a younger sister.

She hugged me and asked Turner to take my bag up to room twenty-one, then walked me around the building. She was nervous about the state of repair. I said the place looked great.

My apartment had a coral couch and chairs, green carpet, and a glass dining table with pointy metal legs. The dishes were scarred plastic, and I got seven tumblers, all different. Nothing matched. One of my lamps had a spacewalk scene on its shade.

"We've got a problem with the oven," she said. She

walked around the apartment opening windows. "You're not going to bake anything, are you?"

"Don't think so," I said. "I guess I ought to say I wish we had come before, Alex and me, when things were better."

"Now's fine," she said. She handed me a tiny deck of cards. "Take a look. They're Japanese. The game's called Hana Fuda. Flower gathering game."

"Pretty," I said, looking at the cards.

We went out, stopping by the indoor pool so I could meet Jane and Dzubas, two other permanent residents. He had his arm in a cast, and she was tattooing a knife on his wrist. They were arguing about salt. Outside it was cooling down but the wind was constant and loud. There was a tanker in the Gulf, outlined against a middle-blue sky. We crossed the street and sat by the edge of the highway. She still had the cards, which were domino-size and thick as shirt cardboard. She told me about them—there was a rain man, there were magic animals, banners, a flying lantern card. The suits were flowers and grasses. I didn't have any idea what she was talking about. "I'm not sure I'm getting this," I said, picking up a card.

She tapped it with the nail of her first finger. "Pampas grass," she said, showing me more cards in the suit. "August. The grass comes to full beauty in August. Watching grass by moonlight is a favorite pastime of theirs."

I closed one eye and raised the other eyebrow at her and that seemed to change something, break some ice. She laughed in a pretty way, sort of like Alex, then picked up the cards, shuffled them together, and slipped them into her jacket pocket.

"Sorry," she said. "I always want these to mean something. A long time ago I really liked this game. When Mel and I were, you know, splitting up." She smiled. "So, what's the story?"

I told her Alex had turned to me during one of those postcard breaks on MacNeil-Lehrer and said she thought we'd be better off if we just forgot the marriage. It came out of nowhere, and I knew it was final the minute I heard it. The more we talked the more lost I felt. I guess I showed Alex too much of that. When I cried she was patient, but I couldn't stop. Everything made me cry. Stuff around the house that looked O. K. before suddenly seemed foreign. When I came around, which was a day later, none of the routines worked. She wasn't interested in charm, anger didn't scare her, my little-boy act got pathetic looks. Everything had changed. After a couple of weeks there was a meeting with her lawyer, a woman named Blaze, who had an accent and enough hair for the three of us. Blaze said she could handle things if I didn't want a lawyer of my own. I said that was fine, then thought better of it and got a guy who looked like Wayne Newton out of the Bar Association's annual directory. I asked him to give Alex what she wanted, within reason. He told me he was ready to rip her apart.

Dominica was sympathetic. I didn't know her at all, but she seemed funny and tough, mannish. She fiddled with her hands while I talked. The wind blew her jacket collar and the sun went down, splashing us with pink light. Somewhere in the middle of the report I stopped thinking of Alex and started thinking of Dominica. I tried not to, but I was comparing them, calculating which was quicker, which prettier, which more gentle. Dominica was winning and I kept thinking, "Take it easy. Don't get stupid here."

She knew what was going on. I guess it must have been obvious. When my talk trailed off she squinted at me, then looked away toward the restaurant sign, tightening her face against a smile. "You're a bad guy, you know that?" she said.

SATURDAY I SLEPT LATE, walked on the beach alone, felt sorry for myself. I'd been thinking of the divorce as sudden, even whimsical, but now, after telling Dominica, it seemed predictable. The beach made things worse, so I spent the afternoon inside, sitting in the room, making occasional trips to the lobby or the pool just to move around. I wasn't so much bothered by the marriage part as I was by the idea of not seeing Alex, not being around her, not having her in the constant way married people have each other.

Dominica came by the room at six to tell me there was a beach party planned and that I had to go.

Half an hour later Dzubas got the little fire going, and a herd of milk cows from a nearby farm wandered down onto the sand. There were a dozen of us out there. We scattered when the cows came, and that scared them, so they started running in circles, bellowing. I hadn't realized how big and mean cows look when they're right next to you. Dominica went in and called the farmer, and he came over with his son and moved the cows. She invited the boy and his father to the party, so they stayed, and the cows stayed too, huddled across the road on the thin grass in back of the motel.

We spent most of the night on the beach. I sat with Dominica, watching, listening to her talk to the residents and guests. I had a fair time. It was nice being with her on the beach and it was O. K. being on my own. Dominica liked it too, and from time to time touched me as if I were her date on a hay ride or something. Once she left a hand relaxed against my knee for a long stint and we both carefully ignored it, but the feeling was alarming—sexy, scary. At three in the morning she walked me to my room. We stood outside the door and shook hands for about five minutes. Before I went to sleep I called Delta's eight-hundred number and canceled my return.

THE NEXT AFTERNOON we made a quick trip to Fort Myers to get these special steaks because a guy named Gil—an old friend of Dominica's who sold carpets for a living—was coming for dinner. We had fun in the grocery store, which was big, glossy, full of beach paraphernalia by the check-out counters. Dominica told me about an article she'd read on the human parts industry. A storm blew up a pretty, dark-green sky as we were driving back to SeaSide. It was pitch black in her apartment when we went in. We slid the bags onto the kitchen counter without stopping to turn on the lights. It was dark enough so that we couldn't see each other. "What is this, the end of the known world?" she said. "Are you hiding?"

I squatted so I could see her against the refrigerator. She got on her hands and knees. "What are you doing down here?" She twisted my ankle and tossed me on my backside.

"Hey," I said. "Georgia Championship Wrestling."

"I don't want my umbilical cords in some old guy's leg, O. K.? That's a new rule."

"It'll never happen," I said.

We played for a few minutes, moving like apes around the room. When my eyes adjusted to the darkness so I could finally see her, she took a swipe at me, then rolled on her back, her arms and legs in the air.

"What is this? Are you quitting?"

"No," she said. "I am not quitting."

An hour later I was still on the couch—we had shoved it up against the sliding doors that looked out on the Gulf—and Dominica was across the room, behind me, splay-legged and leaning against the wall. "I don't know why I have to live with sculptured carpet," she said. "Why can't I have plush, at least?" She walked on her knees to the couch and kissed me.

"Maybe this Gil guy should give you a bunch of carpet. Something in peach, with a fleck. Maybe a couple of flecks."

"Put on the music, will you? I'm doing a pie." She picked up her clothes and headed for the kitchen, and I went to rewind the tape we'd been playing.

Dzubas and Jane came early. He told me what he thought about Gil. "The dude comes around once a year, dressed for syncopation," he said, pointing toward the kitchen. "He's got some major league hopes over here."

"You don't like him because he's big," Jane said. "You hate people bigger than you."

"It's true. I don't like to look at him," Dzubas said.

"It's a painful experience. But it's not just size, it's the rest of it, the carriage. Like women harnessed to their giant breasts."

Jane was on the couch leafing through a magazine. She dropped her jaw and stuck a finger in her mouth as if to gag herself. "He weeps all the time when he sees giant breasts," she said. "I've never seen anything like it. I aways know when some giant breasts are around."

"This is what I get," he said, waving his drink toward her and heading for the kitchen. "It's hard for me to say anything at all."

"You manage," Jane said, watching him go. She slid the magazine onto the table in front of the couch. "So, Mr. Martin. Do you find me hostile?"

"Yes," Dominica called from the next room.

"Hospitals have contracts to buy umbilical cords for twenty-three bucks a pop," I said, "Learned that today. They use them for arteries. It was in the paper."

Dzubas came out of the kitchen with tap water splashed on his cheeks. Jane said, "Not funny, powder brain."

When Gil arrived he was wearing madras pants and carrying three cases of rug samples. We looked at the samples while we had drinks. At dinner I got the corner of the table, with the leg between my knees. Before we started Gil pointed his fork at Dominica and said, "You and Marty there. I guess you're an item?"

"Been at each other for weeks now, Gil," Dzubas said. "Ravishing each other and farm animals too. Cows, pigeons . . ."

"Pigeons aren't farm animals," Jane said.

"Doesn't matter," he said. "Horses next. Horse ravish."

Gil said, "I don't get it."

"This can't be true," I said.

"He's kind," Jane said, leaning back in her chair and flapping her napkin at Dzubas. "Hey. Bozo. You want to settle down?"

When I finished eating I excused myself and went to my room for a nap. About ten-thirty I got up and came back out to see what was going on. Dominica and Dzubas were at the far end of the atrium, looking out at a veiled quarter moon. It was muggy in the building. The Astro-Turf squished under my feet. The air-conditioning hum was deep and constant and one of the fans clicked as it turned. I stretched the skin around my eyes with my fingers and went downstairs. "How is everybody? Gil leave?"

"She went for a thousand bucks worth of savage-brown nylon pile and he split," Dzubas said.

There were searchlights jerking through the sky over in the direction of Lullaby. I said, "Look at that."

"Practicing for Pancake Week," Dominica said, tapping the glass. "Let's take a walk. I need somebody young and attractive and carpet-positive to talk to."

"Two out of three," Dzubas said.

It was chilly out. The storm had slicked everything up. There were puddles around, with lights glittering in them. It smelled like fall, and more rain. The wind got through my shirt. We headed for the Mercedes, which was parked in the lot alongside the SeaSide sign.

"I got a call from Alexandra," Dominica said. She

opened the car and started it, then switched on the radio
and hit a couple of buttons. I heard the computer-like
beep of the station search intercut with squawks of Mexi-
can music. Dominica turned to me, sliding her boots
back and forth on the sandy blacktop. "I feel terrible.
She's lonely. She misses you."

"I miss her," I said, leaning against the fender.

"So what's your program? I mean, I've got leases on all
these outfits. People coming in and everything." She
waved back toward the buildings, then pulled the jacket
collar up around her neck and sat quietly for a minute,
smoking and wagging her head to the radio music.

I said, "I'm doing O. K. here, aren't I? I don't have to
run off."

She made a real hard face and stared at me for a minute, then reached into the car and played with the volume
on the radio until she had it the way she wanted it.


GEORGE TOOLE showed up at noon Monday. He was
supposed to be a developer but he looked more like a
dance hall king—big hair, a nail-head mole on his lip,
aviator-style glasses with thick red lenses. Three of us met
him by the outside part of the pool.

Jane did about half of a cowgirl curtsy and took his
hand. "Howdy," she said.

"That's some hair you got," he said, reaching to touch
Jane's hair, which was red and severely curled.

"Look who's talking," Jane said, dodging him.

Dominica slid her hand over her scalp.

Dzubas came out of the building walking funny, like a

football star. He had been an engineer, but now he had four telephones and an IBM PC, so he was putting out an investment letter for a hundred hopefuls. "What's the story here?" he said.

Jane said, "Mr. Toole, meet Mr. Dzubas, financial adviser to the empire."

Dzubas took a bow, folding his cast into his stomach and going down at the waist. "My pleasure," he said.

Dominica elbowed me. "The monkey comes to visit," she whispered. Then she got an arm around Toole's shoulder and started to lead him away. "Let me show you the layout," she said. "I wasn't calling you a monkey. I was calling him a monkey."

"I understand," Toole said.

"I don't," Dzubas said.

"She likes monkeys," Jane said, banging a knuckle on Dzubas's cast.

Dominica pulled Toole away. They walked out to the edge of the road. We watched her point out the highlights. Toole's little hat followed her gestures up and around the property, across the beach and out to the restaurant, past the piers and pilings, then over the Gulf and back toward town.

"How's the divorce going?" Dzubas said.

"I'll bet he's a geek," Jane said. She tugged my arm and pointed to Toole and Dominica. "This guy, I mean. Not you. He's going to eat something, maybe the pool furniture." She brushed at her arms. "I've got to wash these."

"Big job," Dzubas said. "I'll go with you."

"Nope. I'm taking a rest. I need a rest. P. Rob's

around, why not play with him? Nobody ever talks to him."

"Our social director," Dzubas said, eyeing Jane.

"The social director says, put your hands on your head," she said. "Good. Now, put your hands on your toodle—heh, heh, heh." She patted my back and headed for the building.

We followed her in that direction, but stopped outside by the pool and sat in the redwood chairs with the bright yellow cushions, facing the Gulf. We could see Turner sitting with his suitcase-size radio under a palm tree. Around to the left Dominica was shaking hands with Toole. He stopped and pointed toward the restaurant and she turned and shaded her eyes looking in that direction. It was a non-functioning restaurant, once the Seabird Inn, that she said she was going to reopen one day. Overhead, the clouds looked like metal plates sliding back and forth. In a few minutes Toole got into his Cadillac convertible and drove off. Dominica came our way.

"We've got a silverfish here," she said. "If he's in land development I'll cook him and sell portions."

"She's our top money-maker," Dzubas said. He waved his cast at a fly that was zipping around his face. Then he waved at the fly with his good hand.

Turner cranked the radio up loud and yelled something at us. The music was a tango song and Dominica started a Valentino dance, then quit suddenly. "I wonder if it's Mel," she said, looking down the highway after the Cadillac. "He's Mel's type." She glanced at Dzubas. "What do you think?"

Dzubas shrugged. "Bullfighter down on his gruel."

When Dominica went inside Dzubas started to follow

her, then stopped and said, "The husband's a twit. He plays these little tricks on her. Sends people around. He's a hunter. I don't mean all hunters are twits . . . or maybe I do. You must have known him, anyway."

I nodded and he went in. I had met Mel once, two years before, on the eve of their divorce. Dominica had come to visit us and Mel had followed. What I remembered about him was that he made a lot of anguished faces during an otherwise ordinary conversation.

LATER THAT AFTERNOON I went to find Dominica. I walked around the building a couple of times. No luck. Finally I sat down in the recliner on the balcony, next to the glass, and stared at the jungle out back. There was part of an airplane out there in the brush. War surplus. It was a P-38 Night Fighter—I knew that because I built models as a kid. It had twin fuselages, the nose section in the middle, and a camouflage paint job that looked homemade. Mel had planned to get lots of planes and draw the tourists, but he lost interest. Dominica said she used it as a kind of retreat, sometimes spending days out there.

I'd been sitting half an hour when I saw her go across the clearing and up the boarding ladder. She stood on the landing by the plane's hatch, looking back through the broken trees that separated us. She looked straight at me, but I couldn't tell whether she saw me or the glare of the sunset shooting off the glass. She played nervously with the two or three potted plants on the landing, plucking them, then lit a cigarette and blew smoke into the honeysuckle wrapping down the handrail.

Toole's Cadillac came around the building and rolled

through the dirt toward the plane. He had the top down. He opened the door and jumped out before the car was stopped, and he kind of bumped into the door and bent over favoring his leg. Dominica came down and they stood at the edge of the clearing, talking. She seemed pained, and he gestured a lot, moving his arms around, pointing at things. They were about a hundred yards away. I went downstairs, still watching. I saw Toole bring out something that looked like a toy gun.

I went out and yelled, "Hey," moving toward them. "What's going on here? Is that real?"

He twisted around like one of those robot welders in TV news stories and leveled the thing at me. "Real? You want to see real? Why don't you just hump it on inside?"

I quit walking and stretched my arms out at my sides. "O. K.," I said. I looked at Dominica. "Are you all right?"

She made a face, and I said, "Right. Sorry."

The guy Toole was down in a police crouch. He looked silly, and he wasn't comfortable with the gun. He was wiggling it and twitching his head first at her, then at me. He looked like Dustin Hoffman, for some reason.

He started backing toward his car. The gun was bobbing around, pointing every which way. He said something to Dominica I couldn't catch, then slid into the car seat and pulled the door shut with his left hand. He got the car in reverse and twisted the wheel, running himself backwards in a half-circle into the brush, then he dropped the shift lever and rolled forward. The car was facing me now. I couldn't see the pistol. Then he pulled it up off the seat and pointed it toward the airplane. He fired twice. The shots were slight little things, pops almost, but piercing and insistent, and he jerked in his seat with each one. The bullets pinged when they hit the metal. Then he floored the Cadillac and lurched out to the parking lot and out of sight.

I started for Dominica. She was shaking her head. She said, "We can handle it. This is not a crisis."

I heard tires screeching out front, then another shot, then the whine of the Cadillac engine trying to speed up. "I'm perfectly calm," I said.

"Right," she said. She put her arms around me and turned me toward the motel. "Let's get in here and slow everybody down," she said. "They'll think it's CIA if they get a chance."

Dzubas stuck his neck out his second-story window. "What was that?" he said. "Am I missing it?"

Jane was inside, sitting on the pool apron, her back against one of the chrome ladders. She was laughing. "I'm walking around trying to find everybody and here comes this guy shooting up the place," she said. "So I look out there and—what can I tell you? I saw the whole thing. It's crazy. Who's he shooting at?"

Dominica said, "Nobody. It's just Mel. He entertains me with these little jokes. You know, scary and interesting."

"I'm doing all right," I said. "I'll be fine."

Dominica patted me on the shoulder. "Take it easy. It was kind of funny. Did you see the outfit he had on? He looked like the Lone Ranger or somebody." She wiped my forehead with her palm and said, "You should have seen this one. Tower of strength. It was just, like—shots rang out."

Dzubas came down with a teenage girl I didn't recognize. At the bottom of the stairs he came toward us and she went the other way. A few people put their heads out windows into the atrium, a couple of doors opened, but that was it. The vacationers around the pool collected in two and threes, a few lingering to hear Dominica's account. She went over the story—he'd been yelling about the property, about how dangerous it was for a single woman to be running a resort.

Dzubas shook his head and said, "With a real gun?"

Jane said, "Oh, shut up. I'll real you in about a minute."

Dominica walked with me to my apartment. "I don't want you to worry about this business," she said, playing with a nail in the door frame. "I know what he's doing. I asked him to quit, I even threatened him. It didn't do any good. Once he sent me a death certificate every day for a month. When I get really mad I can slow him down, but that's all. He was sort of like this when we were married, but it's worse now. I should have known when this guy showed up—I did know, really."

We went in and turned on the TV, leaving the sound off, and sat in my living room watching the tail of the news and then the action shows. She told me stories about her marriage. I don't know if it was the matter-of-fact way she told them, or what was in them, or both, but I was terrified. These were horror stories, the kind you read about in the newspaper. I wanted to do something to make her feel better, but there wasn't anything to do but sit and listen. About nine we started to make love but then quit in the middle of things and went for a walk. We got hamburgers at a beach dive called the Rubber Shack that specialized in scuba gear, then went back to the motel. She fell asleep ten minutes into David Letterman.

I went down to the pier. A flood lamp out there was wired to a metal pole attached to one of the pilings. The setup was shaky and rattled a lot in the wind. Dzubas was sitting on the rail smoking a cigar, and there were hundreds of bugs around.

"She swears he won't hurt anybody," he said.

"She told me," I said.

He dropped the cigar into the water and I watched it float sideways under the pier.

"I'm going to bed," he said. "Don't stay all night."

He started for the motel. I watched him all the way to the door, then sat there for a minute with my eyes shut and listened to the Gulf splash against the pilings. The sky was muddy. Sitting out alone wasn't fun, so after a few minutes I got up and started across the beach. Sea-Side was tiny and isolated against the horizon, lit only by its sign, two flood lamps, and dots of yellow—bug lights. It looked frail and mysterious, like a stucco store on a prairie in some amateur painting. The water hissed behind me and, in the distance, a ship's horn echoed. I made a sound mimicking the horn and went across the road and into the building. There was a mist around the pool. It moved with me, gave way around me like smoke, as if it inhabited the building in a proprietary way. I climbed to the balcony and got on my back on the floor, listened to the mooing of the beach wind, felt my weight against the concrete. The concrete was cold. I felt it through my clothes. I felt the shirt creasing across my back and bunching at my waist.

In a few minutes Dominica came out of my apartment.
She didn't see me. She went downstairs and stood by the
pool, wiping sleep out of her eyes. Her movements were
small and quick, circular, her hands going around her face
like little pistons. Seeing her there was eerie, with the
green glow coming out of the water, kind of flickering in
the surrounding darkness, with the click of the fans, the
push of the Gulf wind twisting the building, banging
loose things around, and Dominica alone in the tinted
light, digging at her eyes. It was as if we were on the set of
some strange movie, caught for a second in the middle of
one night.

Cars went by on the highway, going fast, the sound of
them magnified in the open atrium. She started to go in,
then saw me upstairs and said, "Hey. My own personal
gunslinger."

I waved, then decided that wasn't enough, so I sat up
and said, "Yep."

She gave me a wry face and then came up the stairs
and sat with me, looking at the pool water. She put her
arm around me. She bumped me with her shoulder a
couple of times. She said, "Hey. This ain't bad. So,
where's our pistol?"

ALEX CALLED Tuesday. The first thing she said was, "Are you sleeping with her?" Then, without waiting for an answer, she said, "Never mind. I don't care. You two can do whatever you want. I don't have a chain on you."

"I don't know what we're doing," I said. Then, while I listened to the silence on the phone, I shook my head and thought what a silly thing that was to say. I said, "Sorry. It's a reflex. Yes. The answer is yes."

"You're lying," she said. She hung up.

I was alone in Dominica's bed. It was late morning. The sunlight was pale coming through the thick blinds. I knew Alex would call back, so I waited, my hand on the phone. I got it on the first sound. "She's my sister," Alex said. "It's not her fault. It's your fault. You want to hurt me. Well, it won't work. You make my spine twitch, but that's all. I feel sorry for you."

"That's why we're divorced," I said.

"We're not divorced yet. We won't be divorced for another twenty days. I should nail your butt for this. Two days ago I was telling her I missed you—scum. You're scum, you know that?"

"I'm not scum, Alex."

There was dead air on the phone. I was nervous, but I figured if I said anything she'd take it wrong, so I waited.

After a minute she said, "It doesn't mean anything. I mean, missing you. It's true, but it doesn't mean anything. It's just lonely with nobody else around."

"I know the feeling," I said.

"Sure you do," she said. "Sitting over there knee deep in my little sister. Where is she, anyway? Let me talk to her. I don't want to talk to scum anymore. God, I'd like to smash your face, just once."

I asked her to hold on, then tripped as I was climbing off the bed, dropping the telephone receiver in the process. "It's O K.," I yelled at the phone. "I'll get her."

Dominica was in the tiny front room of her apartment, the room she used as an office. She was on the telephone with the pool supply people, so I wrote "Alex" on the yellow pad in front of her and tapped the blinking button on her phone. She nodded, and I went back to the bedroom and waited silently on the line for her to pick up.

When I heard her get on the line I hung up as quietly as I could. I went to my apartment and showered, then sat on a towel on the bed thinking about them being sisters. They didn't seem like sisters to me. They seemed like these two different women. I tried to feel peculiar about being married to one and sleeping with the other, but it didn't work. I could think it, think it was evil, irregular, despicable, but I didn't feel that. I was sorry I hadn't done any better with Alex on the phone and thought I ought to call her back, but then figured that was a bad idea, that I'd make her feel worse. I was lonely too, but all I could think about was what wasn't there any more, which felt awful. I'd lost it. Five years of stuff sucked away, reduced to civility, manners. It wasn't so much what was gone, but what wouldn't be there. Hello, how are you, fine. Always reserved, distanced, hiding. Performing. I'd been through it. The only options you get are wretched. You can be polite, well-meaning, then af-

terwards you think you've been cruel. You can try to re-
capture the intimacy, in a moment standing side-by-side
at a reception for somebody you knew, and you get cut off
for your effort. Or maybe she tries for the intimacy and
you feel repelled—she's pathetic. It ought to work better,
but it doesn't. You cut yourself off and it's gone, whatever
made intimacy possible. I thought of Alex at home,
cross-legged on the couch, wearing my shirt, bitching
about her office, laughing at herself for something she
said, worrying about a letter she wrote for some client. I
thought about the things we could talk about now and
the things that were off-limits, about the way we would
be—like amputated parts, limbs.

Dominica tapped on the bedroom door and then
peeked around its edge. "Naked," she said.

I flipped the ratty-looking comforter over my legs and
said, "Yeah. Sorta."

She pushed into the room but stayed clear of the bed.
"You told her," she said.

"Force of habit," I said. "I don't lie very well anyway.
What'd she say?"

"She was fine. She's coming, though. Here. Tomorrow. I didn't try to stop her." Dominica propped two
window blinds apart with her fingers. "I hate my hair like
this. She'll think I'm crazy. She probably already thinks
I'm crazy. I'm going out back for a while." She walked
quickly across the room, then stopped at the door. "Are
you O. K.?"

"Sure," I said. "I guess."

"She's not staying here. She's renting a car and she
wants to stay in Odalisque. At my competitor's."

"What's Odalisque?" I said, rolling off the bed. "Let

me get dressed and I'll come out with you, I mean, if that's all right."

"A town up the coast. The Hotel Imperial," she said. "In continuous operation since nineteen and thirty-six. It's a strange little town. You'll like it."

"I'll like it," I said.

"Yep. She's meeting you there at six tomorrow night. I'm going to call for the rooms. Get finished and meet me outside, O. K.? We'll check the plane for damage."

WE DIDN'T get to the plane until evening. Dzubas had a crisis and we had to wait for the plumber. Then there was a thunderstorm, one of those quick ones that come up and rattle the windows for twenty minutes, then kind of hang around and turn everything gray for a long time. Then Dominica had to get two families set up—they changed apartments twice each, which was unpleasant.

I was taking a walk when Dominica caught up with me on the beach. "Isn't it great?" she said. "Wouldn't you like to own one of these things?"

She linked her arm in mine and tugged me away from the water, which was shimmering in the late afternoon light. The sun was close to the horizon and completely obscured by clouds turning good versions of rose and copper. I said, "Pretty amazing stuff," and twisted her back around facing the sunset.

"Beginner's luck," she said. "Come on. I'll show you my private plane."

We went back to and then around the motel, across a clearing the size of a weekend softball field, and then into the dense brush. It was darker in among the trees and bushes, and everything was still wet, so things glinted if you caught them right, and the bits of sun that got through flashed on the spider webs woven into the tree limbs. I could see parts of the plane, but I didn't get the whole picture until we reached a much smaller clearing, and then it was sitting there, propped up on railroad ties and fifty-gallon drums. It had a beat up nose with a blue circle hand-painted on the tip, a queer-looking glass cockpit that was an awkward lump on top of the fuselage, and it sat flat, parallel to the ground, like a beached sea cow. The sunset spiraled off the windows and spread like bits of glass through the leaves and vines draped around the place.

Dominica said, "Hang on a minute. Let me get the lights."

She went up the steps and ducked into the hatch. I heard something metal bang against something else, then a generator cranked up and lights came on in the cockpit and down the fuselage, wing lights came on, lights at the tops of the tails.

The effect was like some nighttime picnic in the woods. The plane wasn't really black at all, it was gray, different shades of gray, painted in puzzle shapes with house paint and a brush.

She came out and said, "Well?"

I felt a chill, closed my arms over my chest. "Pretty well, how're you?" It seemed a lot more cut off from the motel than it was. There was only fifty feet of forest between us and the motel's yard, but I felt as though I couldn't be seen from there or anywhere else. I walked under the wing and reached up to trace the numbers that had been painted there, numbers that I could see clearly through the paint job.

Dominica sat down on the top step of the boarding ladder, her elbows on her knees, her chin in hands. I came out from under the wing and grabbed the propeller blade, which wasn't painted and had begun to rust. It was huge.

"Pretty big, isn't it?" she said.

"Pretty nasty," I said. "Usually they're all cleaned up, like toys. This reminds me of those pictures you see of sea creatures nobody knows about—huge, on abandoned-looking beaches, you know? There's always a guy in a red shirt standing beside it, leaning against it with one hand." I stepped on the bottom of the ladder, pulling back and forth on the handrails. "Actually, I've only seen one such picture. In an unexplained phenomena book that I almost bought at the B. Dalton in the mall by our house. Our ex-house. It was Florida, I think. They had its mouth propped open with a four-by-four, and the guy was standing there with his hand on one of this thing's teeth, which were about the size of quart beer bottles. I looked at that for a long time. I guess they must've faked it, but I couldn't tell. I mean, if they found something like that it'd be all over the place, wouldn't it?"

She shrugged at me. "Never saw it. I know what you're talking about, though."

"This thing was big as a bus," I said. "And it had these slits in its side like one of the sharks, but the caption said it wasn't any kind of shark."

"The fish from outer space," she said. "That's perfectly clear. Well known in these parts. One of the much-discussed mysteries from the nineteen fifties."

"I'm getting the book and showing it to you," I said. "That'll settle you down."

"I'm settled, I'm settled," she said. "I just want some coffee. You?"

"You got coffee out here?"

"Yep. I've got Mr. Coffee right inside this door here. Come on up."

She got to her feet and I went up the steps. The inside of the plane had been gutted. I could stand comfortably as long as I stayed more or less in the center of things. Toward the back of the fuselage there was a platform with a couple of old loungers, a coffee table, and a bed on it. I took one of the chairs.

"Melvin started to make an apartment," she said. "You can see he didn't get very far. But I've got a kitchen back here, and this bed—I could live out here if I wanted to."

Two brown fluorescent drafting lamps jutted out from the curved walls on opposite sides of the space. I moved the one that was shining in my eyes, and said, "Might be a bit on the stark side of things, huh?"

She slid a tape into a mini-deck that was on the table and the place was filled with Laura Branigan singing about how she lived among the creatures of the night. "Remember this?" Dominica said. "I loved this when it first came out. She wants to be such a hound, this woman."

I knew the song because I knew the video that had been done to sell it—a rape fantasy, which I thought was a strange kind of promotion for a woman to do these days. "Sold me," I said. "I don't admit that to everybody."

"The secret is safe with me," she said. She was moving a little with the music, measuring the coffee, pouring water. "You're the first one who's been in here, I mean, except me and Melvin. That's strange." She finished with the coffee and sat on the bed, pushing aside the telephone, which was silent, even though lights in the row of lights at the bottom flicked on and off occasionally. "Debelled it myself," she said, touching the phone again.

We sat in silence for a few minutes. I studied the metal of the plane's belly, the curved structural pieces, the rivets, the thick gray paint that covered everything. Even with the drafting lamps it was dark. The small round windows were scarred and warped, rippling the narrow views—in one a tree trunk and a wedge of sky, in another part of a propeller and some foliage. Dominica sat on the edge of the bed with her eyes closed, as if she were fighting a headache. There was a bead of orange light coming from the switch on the coffee maker. The phone lights blinked. I said, "Don't you think maybe it's a little dreary in here? You want to go up to the cockpit?"

"You go ahead," she said. "I'm just resting a minute. I may take a nap. You want to take a nap?"

The coffee-maker gurgled. I said, "Nap? What about Alex? What about Toole? If we both take a nap, who's going to worry?"

"Right," she said. "Get after it. I'll be right here." I watched her stretch out on the bed. "I called Mel," she said. "He asked me if I wanted him to talk to the police. He called me sweetie all during the conversation. It was horrible the way he said it. I can't imagine why I ever married him, you know what I mean? I mean, what was I thinking?"

A reddish spider with extraordinarily long legs and a body the size of a silver dollar crawled along the arm of the second chair. I said, "We've got a visitor here. Spider."

"On the chair?"

"Yes," I said.

"That's Wally. Leave him alone. He's a friend."

"I wasn't going to hurt him," I said, getting out of my chair. "I'm not great on spiders, though. You want to, uh, take care of this?"

She propped herself up on her elbows. "You're afraid of spiders? We're going to have to call this thing off if you're afraid of spiders." She slid down and off the bed, went to the chair with the spider in it, and crouched down close to the arm. The spider stopped moving. "Hiya, Wally," she said, flattening her hand in front of it. "How's things? You want to go for a ride on the big airplane?"

"I'm going to die now," I said. "You aren't putting it on your hand, are you? Oh, Jesus."

She poked the spider's back legs, and it obediently crawled forward into her palm. She flew her hand around the room a couple of times, then carefully walked toward the front of the plane and put the spider outside the entry hatch. "Don't get crazy out here," she said.

"I don't think you ought to be talking about crazy," I said, when she was back in bed.

"Oh, it's nothing," she said. "I'm just at one with nature, is all. You want to climb up here on the bed or what? You waiting on a comet? Come on." She slapped the bed a couple of times.

I crouched down too much as I went for the bed, tripping

on the tiny throw rug, and lurching onto the mattress.

"Hang on," Dominica said. "I thought we were tired."

She gave me a dry kiss on the forehead and then moved to the far side of the bed. In a few minutes she was asleep, her breathing slow and steady. I lay on my back and stared at the round windows, thinking about Alex. Rain started pinging on the fuselage, on the wings, patting on the foliage outside.

I WOKE UP alone. For a second I thought it was morning and I didn't remember where I was, and I looked for Alex. Then I remembered. Dominica wasn't there. My neck hurt. I twisted up on the bed and sat a minute, kneading the back of my neck. I went to the cabin hatch and looked out. It was night. The lights around the plane made it spooky, but through the trees I could see the motel and the highway in a creamy moonlight. I went down the steps and crunched through the leaves toward the motel. I was about halfway there when I saw Dominica standing in the parking lot with a uniformed policeman. The guy's car was there, interior lights on because his door was open. The police radio squawked a couple of times. The cop had a cigar.

I crossed the grass to the building. Turner was just inside the glass, watching Dominica and the cop, wearing a gold and black plaid shirt and a red leather beanie. I said hello when I went in.

"Why, howdy there." His speech was slow and had a kind of mechanical lilt to it, tripping into falsetto on off-beat syllables. It was fascinating and slightly unsettling to hear him talk. "You been keeping an eye on my lights?" He waved toward the sky. "Next week's the week. You be around? Got a special on grape waffles."

"Sounds good," I said. "I'm looking forward to it."

"She likes you is the way I hear it," he said, smearing his cuff against the glass. "Took you out to the Flying Tiger and everything. That's special, boy."

"Uh-huh. What's with the police?" I cocked my head toward the parking lot.

"The guy just showed up," he said. "We were in here talking about my party and the guy drives up with his blue lights flashing. No siren though. It always scares me when they use the lights without the siren, they're so quiet then, you know what I mean? They kind of whiff by you." He did the whiff sound a couple of times so I'd get the idea. "I think it's O. K., though. After yesterday. She didn't call them?"

I glanced out the window. "I don't know."

"I figured she'd want to take old Mel down one of these days," he said. "He's been beating up on her for a time. Not that she can't take it."

"It's more likely she'd call a lawyer, isn't it?"

"Might," he said. "Course, Mel's a lawyer himself. She may not have the highest regard for the lawyers. Might get her in trouble, too." He eyed me, thin hair poking out around the edge of his cap, his nose squinching and unsquinching like a rodent sniffing food. "Don't get me wrong, I like the woman. She's doing fine. She's a rugged item."

"Yes sir," I said. "That I noticed." I turned to look at the kids who were splashing around in the shallow end of the pool. They were Korean, or Vietnamese—slick little black heads bobbing in and out of the water. When they laughed they sounded shrill and nasal. The parents, decked out in Bermuda shorts and sunglasses, squatted at the edge of the pool, admonishing the kids with fierce determination.

"So I hear her sister's coming down," Turner said. "Not staying with us, either. I don't know why. What, we're not good enough for her? She's staying in Odalisque, is what I hear. I was over there one time. Didn't stay long. They don't have any kind of pancake store at all over there. I don't know how they get along."

I started to slap him on the back, but then stopped in mid-swing and waved my hand awkwardly. "Folks probably make them at home," I said. "You know—Bisquick, Log Cabin—the whole thing." I took a step back and winked at him.

"Aren't as good that way," he said. "We make 'em from scratch. We'd never use a mix. I don't like their hygiene practices, I mean the manufacturers. They don't care about pancakes. If a rat falls in the pot, they don't care, they just stir it up some more. Put some cardboard in. Don't get me wrong, cardboard's all right. I read an article about some cows that were fattened up on cardboard, and they were fine. They were real good. But I don't ever use no mix. My people would know right away, one bite, and they'd be after me then, I'm telling you."

I was ten feet away and moving farther, going backward. "I'm looking forward to next week."

"We'll take care of you," he said. "Make you a monster-jack if you want. That's a big guy." He held his hands out in front of him to show me the size. "Got everything in it. I think I may get a patent—it's like a pizza, you know? You can put anything in it there and it's just as good. You can put ice cream in there if you want. You like plums? We can fix you up."

I waved again and then turned around and headed upstairs to my rooms. When I looked back, Turner was still by the glass watching Dominica. I went in and took off my shirt, washed my face, rubbed some fresh water through my hair. Then I put on a clean shirt and slid my feet into the red espadrilles that were a gift from Dzubas, who had ordered eight pairs in two different sizes from an outfit in Maine. The ones he gave me were too small for him. I leaned close to the living room window so I could see the spot in the parking lot where Dominica and the cop were talking. It looked as if they were about finished. He was in the car. She was pulling the door back and forth.

When he left she headed over the highway for the beach. There weren't any lights there except for the lamp on the pier, but the moonlight was almost bright enough to see by. She walked straight across the beach to the edge of the water. I switched off the spacewalk lamp so I could see better, but when I got back to the window I couldn't find Dominica. There wasn't anyone on the beach. There were some people on this side of the road, some kids it looked like, standing around outside of a van, but that was it. She could've gone up the beach, toward Lullaby. In that direction I couldn't see more than a hundred yards before the scrub line cut off my view. On the other side there was the restaurant pier. Beyond it, the beach faded quickly in darkness.

I was struck by the idea that Alex had never talked

about Dominica, that I was her brother-in-law and knew nothing about her except what I'd learned since I arrived. I went outside, down the steps and across the road, and when I got to the beach I ran a little, then stopped running when Dzubas's shoes got stuck in the sand. The wind was stiff and noisy. I went toward the spot where I'd last seen her. It wasn't that dark out there, except for the water. I could see the beach in both directions for a good distance, but she wasn't on the beach. I yelled her name a couple of times. No answer, but that wasn't surprising since she wouldn't have heard me unless she was very close. Some kids from a van had come across onto the beach and were setting up camp a short distance away. I could barely hear their voices in the wind and surf—they sounded like sparrows.

Then, fifty feet in front of me, Dominica stood up in the dark water. She was waving, motioning for me to come in. I parked my shoes and waded toward her. The water was shallow, but there were sand bars, so one minute I was ankle deep, the next I was up to my hips and the breakers were yanking me around.

I grabbed for her arm and both of us fell down, but it was only a foot deep there, so we could sit and not get swamped by the waves. I got a mouthful of salt water anyway.

She said, "I'm taking a swim, here. What's with you?"

We sat in the water for a few minutes, but the surf was too heavy for relaxing, so I got up and pulled her to her feet. "You think we could go in and do something like, uh, watch television?" I said. She didn't hear me, so I repeated it, yelling the second time.

"What's on?" she yelled back.

What was on wasn't very intriguing. She told me that the cop had come on his own, that they'd gotten an anonymous call about a shooting. She knew the cop, so she told him the story. The cop knew Mel, so he believed it. He said there wasn't anything she could do unless she was ready to try to get him on harassment, and that would involve an investigation. They'd have to find Toole and link him to Mel. The cop had wanted to see the death certificates, but she told him she'd thrown them away. "I told him Melvin wants the place back," she said.

"Is that what he wants?" I said. I was watching a very old woman on TV who had a house made entirely out of different kinds of bottles.

"That's part of it," she said. "The rest of it is he doesn't want me to do O. K. without him. For years he hasn't wanted me to do O. K. without him. It's a little crazy."

"You'd think he'd get with the program after a while," I said. I switched the channels around to see what else was on. Some people were praying hard on the Christian network, so I stopped there for a minute. They were really grimacing as they prayed. "We could try this," I said, waving the remote control toward the set.

"I try it now and then," she said. "Sometimes it makes me feel better. It's stupid, but when I watch these people I want to be nice to them. I wish they'd be a little more private."

"I want to read you this letter from a little boy named Jimmy," I said. "His daddy prayed and the power of the Lord blessed them with a new Sony Betamax."

"That's not on TV," she said. "That's the guy who sends those yellow sheets around—the Evangelical Church of the Modern Subdivision, or something like that. We get those."

"So what else has Mel done recently?" I said. "What have I been missing?"

"Let's see . . . he sent a construction crew, a stripper, I'll bet a dollar he sent the wrestlers—did you hear about them? Huge guys. They were here last week or something. Anyway, you see people who look wrong hanging around sometimes. I get a lot of crank calls. Somebody dumped glass all over the beach one time, that may have been him. It's unnerving. What I don't like is that he knows where I am. I mean, I really do think he's gone nuts. That's a pressure. It's tiny, way in the back of your mind, but it's there. Something odd goes on and you think of him. I'm going to have to do something sooner or later. I don't know what."

"Who handled your divorce?" I said. "Couldn't you go back to him?"

"Her," she said. "I was doing something for my people. She preached solidarity and slept with his lawyer. One of them. I don't blame her though. The guy was good. If he'd been my lawyer I'd have slept with him too. In fact, I'd have slept with him anyway. If he walked in that door right now I'd . . ." She leaned over and kissed me alongside the eye, drawing her lips toward my nose. "Just kidding," she said. "I'd blow him away. Put his ham in the slam. Intoxify his armature. And some other stuff."

"Oh yeah?"

"Hide in the bathroom. Stuff like that." She shut her eyes and lay her head on my chest. "Are we pretty nervous about tomorrow? Alex? Or are we prepared?"

"Nervous." I closed my eyes and felt the weight of her against me. She was heavier than Alex, more solid. I said, "You feel good. I hate it when women fold up like butterflies in your arms."

She pulled her head back and raised an eyebrow. "Are you saying I'm not butterfly-like?"

"You're a big butterfly," I said. "Maybe prehistoric, from time immemorial. Is this disgusting?"

"Only slightly," she said. "If you be real nice and shut up for a minute, maybe I'll grease down and hit some poses for you. Do some power lifts. Knock you silly."

"Sounds great," I said.

"Stuff it," she said.

IN THE MORNING I sat in my room and watched the beach glow. More people than usual were out, sunning themselves, playing games with balls, flying colorfully grotesque bat kites, walking, jogging. Dzubas was fishing under the pier. The screen in my window popped in and out noisily as the breezes changed. After a time, movements on the beach became small blurs against the green water, the white sky. I figured Alex had no business divorcing me and less business looking in on me and Dominica. I was angry. I wanted Alex hurt, I wanted to hurt her when I saw her. She always complained that I was too understanding, so now maybe I wouldn't be so understanding, I'd just be getting along with her sister.

Let her sit on that for a while. I reminded myself how unattractive it was to think this way, but it didn't do any good—how about a small dinner party, just the three of us, me and Dominica, and Alex? Then I thought that the fact of the matter was that I hadn't wanted the divorce, and that I might as well admit it, and act like it, and let it alone. I would stay a week, maybe more at Dominica's place. I didn't think I'd want to stay longer than that—too much beach condo life, too many visitors, travellers, all having too much fun, on a budget. And Alex. That made my little romance with her sister smaller.

Jane and Dominica knocked and then came in without waiting for an invitation. I was in the chair by the window, my feet up on the sill. "He's brooding," Jane said. "We've got to get out of here." She stopped halfway across the room and tugged at Dominica's shirt sleeve.

I looked at her and smiled. "What are you, psychic?"

"No. It's just written all over you like a ton of bricks," she said. "Wait a minute . . ."

Dominica stood behind me and played with my hair. "I wish I had some of this," she said. "I don't know what persuaded me to scalp myself."

"MTV," Jane said. "The crippling effects of." She sat on the couch, facing me. "If I had a man like this I'd strap him to the bed. I wouldn't divorce him. That'd be dumb. He's a perfectly good man, isn't he?"

"That's my thought," I said. "Are you guys here to cheer me up or what?"

"We don't know," Jane said. "We're your support system. She's supporting that end, and I'm supporting this end. Got supports at both ends."

Dominica said, "Now you're depressing me, too, Jane."

"Oops. Sorry," Jane said. "I know. Me too. I feel like you're going to the doctor for some major tests."

I shook my head and lowered my eyes at her. "Thanks."

She got up and pulled her hair back with her hands. "O. K.," she said. "I'm out of here. I'm history."

When the door shut behind Jane, Dominica said, "You want me out, too?"

I reached back and touched her hand, which was lightly resting on my neck. "I don't know," I said. "Your hands are cool."

She said, "What are you telling Alex?"

"I'll tell her she's a terrible person, that I don't deserve this cruel and habitual punishment, that I'd like to beat some sense into her, that she owes me a bundle of money for carrying her all these years, and another bundle for educating her, that she's being real stupid, that she's a moron, that I loathe the day I met her and that I don't even remember what that day was, that you screw better than she does and I love it—"

"Oh," Dominica said, nodding. "The usual."

"I'm afraid so. I hate her coming. I hate getting to know you in this situation."

"Does put a color on it, doesn't it?" She went to the window and leaned against the wall, looking out and absentmindedly tracing her fingertips along the curve of my ankle. "Still. Something's better than nothing. Speaking from my point of view, of course."

"And mine," I said. "Count me in. I'm behind you one hundred percent on that."

"I'd like to get you behind me one hundred percent."

"Hold on, now."

"Don't look at me. That was Amy. She lives in here, too." She tapped herself on the chest. "I can't control her. Amy says the most horrible things." She slapped my foot and then pushed it off the window sill. "I don't think it's healthy, you sitting here this-a-way. Why don't you A, take a bath, or B, call your office—that works some-times—or C, go outside where the air can get to you."

I dropped the other foot. "What about yourself?"

"I figure to make myself scarce for a spell. You know where I am. I've got paperwork to do. Here are the keys, and here," she said, pulling a Gulf Oil map out of the back pocket of her jeans, "here is a map to the so-called treasure, pardon the expression."

I took the keys and the map and then held her hand a minute, pressing her knuckles to my cheek. She moved the hand away slowly, caressing my face.

I TOOK THE drive slow. Odalisque was less than fifteen miles away, but I dragged out the trip for half an hour. It was late in the day and I was going away from the sun, so there were lots of long shadows on the highway and shiny reflections in the car windshield. The light seemed to be draining out of the sky. When I got to Odalisque I drove up and down a couple of streets, then found the right one and pulled into a dirt lot alongside an old white two-story house that had a red neon "Hotel Imperial" hung at a slant over the porch steps. Inside, I introduced myself to a woman with twisted, mousy hair who was sitting in an aluminum lawn chair alongside the registration desk. She was in her twenties, wearing black pants, tight at the calves, and a black T-shirt with "Gator Country" across the chest in glitter. She went behind the desk, pulled two keys off hooks, and slid them across the counter, pointing up the stairs with her free hand. "Six and eight," she said. "Towels in the dresser. We're plenty clean here, so don't be fussing with the mattresses. There's a diner two fronts down, or you can eat with Boxer and me at seven, take your choice."

I took the keys and went up. The room was plain—a double bed with a painted metal frame, a sky-blue dresser, a small mirror in an ornate frame painted white, a couple of straight-back chairs. There was a bay window in the thick frame wall. Outside were housetops and the flat roofs of some commercial buildings, and, farther away, jetties, men on tilted docks bent over thin fishing poles. Below there was a street that could've been used in a movie about the thirties. A kid with an orange ball the size of a lemon stood in the doorway of a plumbing shop across the street. A few old people in Hawaiian shirts and floppy straw hats went up and down the sidewalk. Two ragged-looking women were arguing in a vacant lot next to the plumbing store, and, in the street in front of them, a well-dressed man stood on the curb with a steel bucket and tossed water on the taillights of his car. Here and there dogs sprawled, their legs stacked up like so many walking sticks discarded at the ball. It was gray and cooling quickly outside, the way coast towns do at dusk, and the sticky air smelled like fish.

I looked at the second key and realized that when Alex arrived she wouldn't be able to get into her room, so I went downstairs to give the key back to the woman at the desk. She was talking to a thin guy with shoulder-length hair. The guy was wearing a checked flannel shirt and his head was half-covered with bandages. There was a rectangular thing the size of a small cigarette pack under the bandages, behind his left ear. They were arguing about something. He kept motioning toward the thing on his head, tapping it a couple of times, as they talked.

I was behind him, so I waited until the woman could see me, then held up Alex's key. "Is it O. K. if I leave this for my wife?" I said.

The guy spun around and snapped the key out of my hand. "Hey," he said. "Don't let us get in your way here, buddy. We're talking brain surgery, that's all. A couple of peons, like we were in Nam. We're worried about your wife, too. This is my wife," he said, rattling the key at the woman. He didn't look angry. His face was placid, expressionless. He held his hand out toward the woman, then looked at her, looked back at me, then rattled the key again. "Her name's Isabel. We're happy together."

"I didn't mean to interrupt," I said, holding my hands up.

"So why did you?" he said. "Goddamn tourists come around and want to treat you like a goddamn gook, well, I've had about enough. I'm not a gook. She's not a gook. We're Americans. Both of us."

"I'm sorry," I said. I backed away from him, but he moved too, so I stopped where I was.

"Sure you are," he said. "But you'd be sorrier if I ripped the lids off your eyes, wouldn't you?"

Isabel came out from behind the desk and latched onto her husband's arm. She was chuckling. "Boxer's playing with you," she said. She patted his arm. "Aren't you, Boxer?"

"Sure am," he said. "That's what I'm doing. Uh-huh."

She took the key from him. "I'll put this on its hook," she said to me. "When your wife comes I'll give it to her, how's that?"

"That's very gracious of you," I said. "Thanks." I stepped around Boxer toward the door, suddenly conscious of how small the entry was. I said, "I was thinking about taking a walk."

"Shoot," he said. "You want us to take it for you?"

I looked at him. Still no expression. Isabel had hung up the key and was sitting in her lawn chair again. "Sure is pretty out there this time of day," she said. "You be on the lookout, though. We've got a gang of Mexicans beating up folks recently."

"Great," I said. "The diner's this way?" I pointed toward where I thought the water was.

"Right," she said. She kicked Boxer's leg. "Oh, sit down, for God's sake. You're finished." She waved at me, then popped her husband on the head, on the little box under the bandages. "We've got some problems here," she said. "This sucker's way out of whack. You're acting like a gorilla."

He grinned and scratched at his underarms.

I went out, carefully holding the screen door so it wouldn't disturb anyone when it closed.

The juke box in the diner was playing trumpet music—Herb Alpert and the Tijuana Brass, or somebody like that. There were only two people in the restaurant, a scrawny waitress in a pink uniform, and a guy in a golf shirt who was sitting by the grill reading *Basketball Digest*. I took a window booth and ordered coffee.

"You'd better have some eggs," the waitress said, scribbling on her pad.

"Just coffee," I said. "I'm waiting for somebody."

"Side of ham," the woman said, writing again.

"Wait a minute. I want coffee. Black. That's it. No eggs, no ham. All right?"

She turned to the guy by the grill. "I want two up and be nice to 'em, large ham, ring o' browns." She turned back to me. "How about some biscuits?"

I got out of the booth and went to the counter. "I didn't order any of that," I said. "I don't know what this woman's doing, but all I wanted was a cup of coffee."

"Who you calling 'this woman'?" the counter guy said, barely looking up from his magazine.

"Never mind," I said. "I don't want anything. Thank you very much."

The waitress was by the door. "We've a great peach melba," she said. "Huh? Sound good? Take it with you?" She frogged her eyebrows at me and yelled, "Gimmie a peach on the road."

I went up the street and found a soft drink machine at a drugstore. I bought an orange drink and the newspaper, and went back up the sharp hill to the hotel to wait for Alex.

Isabel was alone in the lobby, breast feeding a red-faced baby. "This is Miguel," she said, adjusting the child's head against her breast. "I'm sorry about Boxer. He's got to go to Tampa and have that item looked at. The doctors, they practice on people like us. Anyway, he's due. Boxer is." She pointed to the back of her head. "That's the VA for you. He's got wires in his gray matter, five-year battery, some kind of plutonium or something—it's supposed to keep him stable so he don't bust up me and Miguel. An experimental thing. They've only used it on dogs."

"Uh-huh," I said. I checked the hooks on the wall to see if Alex had arrived. Her key was still there.

"Course, he can't go swimming. That's a shame, too, us being right here by the Gulf and everything. Sometimes I take him and Miguel down there and let 'em get their feet wet, you know what I'm saying? But that's it. That's as far as it goes." The child started hiccupping and her nipple slipped out of his mouth. She grabbed the breast. "Hey," she said to him. "What's a'matta you? Get ova here."

Alex knocked on my door at nine. I let her in. "How are you?" I said.

"Tired," she said. "Who picked this place? My crazy sister picked this? What, they don't have Holiday Inns in Florida? I'm not staying here, you know that, don't you? I'm driving back to that other place, Fort Myers, before I'm staying here. I can't believe this."

"I got here early," I said. We walked around each other in my room as if we were in a hospital and some intimate friend was in grave danger on an operating table two doors down. She looked wrinkled. She had on a suit, a brown two piece thing with a silky blouse, and it hadn't travelled well. I said, "Are you serious? About leaving?"

"You bet," she said. She was peering out the open window at the street below. "Did you see this Invisible Man guy? Jesus."

"You want to go to SeaSide?"

"I do not. Isn't there another hotel in this town? I can't believe Dominica's doing this to me."

I sat down on the corner of the bed. "I think this is it," I said. "Did you see anything on the highway?"

"When I left the airport I saw a blonde in a leotard hitch-hiking and that's all. The rest of the time I was watching for snakes. I mean, it's pitch black out there. What I wouldn't give to be at home in bed right now. Shit."

She went into the bathroom and washed her face and hands.

When she came out I moved to one of the chairs. "So," I said.

"Yeah. I don't believe you either." She sighed and tossed the towel she was using onto the bed. "What're you doing coming down here and humping my sister? Just like that? Doesn't she have enough trouble as it is? Don't we?"

"It isn't like that, Alex. I mean, it is, but we get along. I like her. It doesn't help, you running down here like this, playing the I-don't-know-what."

She frowned at me. I could see that I didn't need to work at hurting her, that was already done. There was a breeze rippling the curtains, shifting her hair. She'd taken off the jacket and I could see lace through the blouse. She didn't look at me, she kept looking out the window. "I am the you-don't-know-what," she said. "I didn't want to be, but I can't help it. I don't want her touching you."

I got out of the chair and started for her, but she glanced up, then shook her head. "Don't be coming over here," she said.

I got her jacket and folded it over the back of one of the chairs. Then I sat on the corner of the bed again. "Did you eat?"

"Not hungry," she said. "I hate to eat. I never do it. It's so much trouble. Food weighs so much."

She laughed. It was a nervous, light laugh, and its sound mixed with the constant noise in a way that sent shivers up my spine. I lifted my shoulders and listened to the bones cracking in my back. Alex came away from the window and sat down on the bed next to me. She said, "So maybe it'll rain."

She had remarkable eyes. We sat for a minute, looking at each other, shoulders barely touching, and the shivers came again. I smiled at her, about the situation, about there being nothing to say. We had some kind of lovely moment, and then she smiled and started combing my hair with her fingers, watching what she was doing. That gradually turned into a kind of child-like lovemaking that I had forgotten, a catalog of affections, without urgency or awkwardness. She wasn't Alex any more. She was someone I didn't know and wouldn't know. Later, when she fell asleep in my arms, it was early morning, well before dawn. There was sea air in the room, skittish rain outside. Shadows of vapor lamps jackknifed up the wall and across the ceiling. I lay awake memorizing the light, the gnawing sweetness in the air, the hiss and clap of the surf, the flapping curtains, the placement of her blouse on the blue chest of drawers.

IT WAS NOON when I woke up. Alex was already dressed, sitting by the window with coffee in a tan cup, reading the paper I'd bought the night before. "This is an amazing thing," she said, rattling the paper. "They discovered a lot of bodies around here—two in the last month." She stopped and thought for a minute. "Maybe I shouldn't tell you this first thing."

I went into the bathroom and closed the door. Her travel kit was neatly alongside mine on the dressing table. I opened the bag and fingered the sample-size bottles of Clinique, the witch hazel, the tiny jar of cuticle cream, the wooden sticks she used on her nails, the file in the mocha plastic sleeve. I remembered all this stuff. After a minute I snapped the kit back together and ran water in the tub. I took a fast bath, slicked my hair back, then wrapped a towel around my waist and went back into the bedroom and got a fresh pair of jeans out of my overnight bag. "Ready," I said. "They discovered the first body . . ."

"In a cardboard box on the sidewalk. This box was there at least a week. Everybody thought it was everybody else's, the box, I mean. It was a brand-new box for an oven. The second one was on a beach. He looked like a sunbather—towel, sunglasses, radio. The guy was laying there in a striped bathing suit. A woman drove by three days in a row and then told the police. Can you believe that?"

I put on a white shirt and left the shirttail out. "How long have you been up?"

"Since eleven. I was downstairs and the guy with the bandages—is his name Boxer? He and his pal—the one who looks like Sam the Sham and the Pharaohs?—they wanted to show me the town. I told them we were on our way out." She folded the paper and dropped it on the floor beside her. "I want to see Dominica. I called her."

Odalisque looked different in the morning than it had in the evening. Maybe I was nervous because Alex was seeing it too. The highway south was like a death row for burger joints. The parking lots had a lot of crackweed and debris in them, the signs were tattered, all the trees were limp and brown. About a mile out we passed a woman standing alongside a black Audi. She was picking at her lip, it looked like, and she didn't make any move to flag us. I turned as we went by, but all I could make out was that her plates were Texas. Another mile and we passed

some farm boys on Ford tractors, old ones, heading toward town. The landscape seemed shallow and dry, and
the sky was huge. I wondered how long Alex planned to
stay. She was behind me in her rented car, a silver sedan
of some kind, Mercury, I think. For a while I watched her
closely in the rear view mirror, but then I didn't pay
much attention. I found a station on the radio and turned
it down low, so that the music wouldn't drown out the
hypnotic sounds of the engine, the tires, the wind. I was
thinking of the difference between Alex's breasts and
Dominica's breasts. Their breasts were completely different. It was an odd thing. I don't know why I thought
their breasts should be more alike. I was laughing at myself for coming up with the idea when I checked the mirror again and Alex wasn't in it. Nobody was back there. I
started to slow, but suddenly Alex came alongside me on
the left, her sedan's engine whining like a jet. She wanted
to race. I looked at her and swung a hand back and forth
to say no. She laughed at that, and punched her accelera-
tor a couple times, making the rented car buck like a low
rider. I checked the speedometer. We were doing sev-
enty, a little more. There wasn't any other traffic on the
highway. She swung her car toward mine then swung it
away, then repeated the move. The next time she did it I
swung with her, going over on the shoulder of the road,
spraying gravel up behind me, then following her across
to the other side, where she went off into the shallow
ditch. I could see her bouncing and laughing in the
sedan. I flipped up the volume on my radio, and started
swiveling on the road in time with the music. She followed me, slipping in behind, and we went snake-like
down the highway.

Then I pulled off on the right shoulder, slowing to about five miles an hour, still rocking the car around. I rolled my window down to let some air in. She was swaying more than I was, but then I made a U-turn and started going back the way we'd come. I was still trying to keep time with the music, which was Latin sounding, so after the U-turn I did a complete circle. She'd stopped when I looped her, but now she came after me, circled right in in front of me, facing me, and we did a car tango—forward and back, circles and half-circles, rocking the cars with the brakes and the gas, all in time with this radio music. I don't know how we managed to miss each other, but we did. We stopped once to let a truck go by, then tried an S-like thing which I did going backwards, but the Mercedes slid sideways on the gravel and I ended up in the ditch. She stopped on the shoulder next to me, facing the wrong way. She grinned and then did a short squirt in reverse as sort of a curtsy, nodding at me from the driver's seat.

I did the best bow I could do without getting out of the car. Then we got back on the road and stayed under the speed limit all the way to Lullaby.

DOMINICA HAD an apartment ready for Alex. It wasn't near mine. It was like mine, but it was on the other side of the pool and downstairs. I sat with them for a few minutes, but then excused myself. Dominica came out with me, standing by the door, shielding her eyes with her hand. She was wearing white shorts and a red blouse that was open at the neck. "It went O. K.?" she said. "You look like you're getting along."

"It was fine," I said. "Except for Boxer and Isabel, not to mention the local diner. I don't think you need to sweat the Hotel Imperial."

"You didn't like it?" she said. She looked genuinely hurt. "Too strange?"

"It was all right. We got through it." There were a lot of kids in the pool playing with a beach ball. Their shouts echoed in the atrium. I turned around and looked them over. "New guests," I said.

"That's not all," she said. "Look at this."

She handed me a Polaroid. It was a picture of a woman in what looked like a hotel room. There was a hotel-type seascape on the wall behind her—one of those with the orange sky and the seagull. The woman had long brown hair and she sat on the edge of the bed holding her shirt open, showing her brassiere, which was plain, flesh-colored. A head-on photo of a snake's head had been carefully cut out and glued over her face.

"I guess this is somebody I know," I said, holding the snapshot up in front of her as if comparing her to the woman in the picture.

"Yeppers," she said. "That's your friend me, some years back. A premarital spree in Miami Beach. I don't know how he got it, though. He didn't take the picture. He wasn't even there. I was with a guy from Georgia, a short-term thing."

"Oh," I said. "This came today?"

She nodded, then peeked back inside Alex's door. "No message," she said. "Just the picture in a homemade envelope. I'm thinking I've had about enough. I should worry about this, shouldn't I?"

"Maybe not—he never comes around here, right? Mel? I mean, you never see him?"

She shook her head. "I never see him."

DOMINICA PLANNED a dinner for the three of us. Late in the afternoon I went into town for wine, and they went somewhere to get veal, pasta, and mushrooms for Alex's special dish. We met back at Dominica's apartment at five-thirty. They were wearing jeans and T-shirts, and dressed that way they looked more alike than I had thought. They laughed and talked in the kitchen, drinking the wine and cooking, and I watched the news on television. When dinner was ready the first bottle was already gone, so we started the second. I pulled back the shades and opened the sliding doors at the end of Dominica's living room so we could see the Gulf and the sunset. I didn't say much during the meal. I didn't think I had to get in on the conversation all the time, and I didn't feel particularly left out, but I was uneasy. I spent my time wondering if Alex was doing a show for me, or for her sister, or if she really was lonely like she'd said on the phone.

About halfway through dinner Alex opened the third bottle of wine. The sun was down but the sky was still full of milky light, and it started raining outside, which was real pretty. It was slow, steady rain that brought a mist, or steam off the pavement and the building, and caught different colored lights—taillights, lights on the building, neon from nearby signs. They were talking and I was watching all this stuff out the window when they started having a fight. I didn't know what had started it, I hadn't heard the conversation. I said, "Hey. What's the problem?"

"We're talking about who's not fucking who any more," Alex said. "Twit."

Dominica covered her face with her hand. "It's me," she said. "In a continuing saga of evil."

"It's not the first time," Alex said.

Dominica stood up and marched around the table to where I was. She crossed herself and said, "Bless me Martin, for I have sinned. I screwed my sister's boyfriend in the tenth grade—wait a minute. I mean, in the tenth grade I screwed my sister's boyfriend. His name was Kyle Greenway. He was a baseball player and my sister's boyfriend at the time."

"If you people are really doing this I'm going to take my ball and go home," I said.

"Take your wick," Alex said. "That'd be more to the point."

"Point?" Dominica said, twisting her face into a parody of astonishment, Rowan and Martin style. "I hadn't noticed that." She picked up her plate and went into the kitchen.

"Slut," Alex said. She threw her napkin at Dominica's back.

"Come on, Alex. Ease it up, will you?" I reached out to touch her arm, but she pulled away.

"Plug it in your ear," she said. "She's a sweat box, always has been. Every time somebody came around to see me, out she'd prance in her panties." Alex got up and did a peculiar-looking hop across the room, then put on a little girl voice. "Oops. I didn't know you were here. See my panties? Aren't they pretty?"

Dominica was standing in the kitchen door, leaning against the jamb. "Oh, Jesus," she said. She got more plates off the table and took them away.

"True," Alex said. She slumped into the couch, her knees kicked out awkwardly in opposite directions. "What about that guy from the radio station?" she yelled to Dominica. She got a puzzled look on her face and rubbed a knuckle into her eye. "What was his name? I forgot his name. He had dark hair."

"He was a DJ. Wait a minute," Dominica said, coming back in. "His name was Peter, wasn't it?"

"He may have been Peter to you," Alex said, raising an eyebrow at her sister. "But I just called him Meat."

"I think I'm starting to spot," I said. I got up and moved toward the balcony. "I'm standing out here in the rain while you guys work this out."

"You're the pits, you know that?" Alex said. "It's your fault. My sister has no control." She was giggling, eyeing Dominica, motioning for her to come over to the couch.

Dominica put the bowls she was holding back on the table and joined Alex. "I'm helpless," she said. "I see a man and I go all weak in the knees."

"That's not a knee, Dominica," Alex said. She hugged her sister, bringing their foreheads together, and whispered something, a story or something, that I couldn't make out, and when she finished they both started laughing, at first a little, then hopelessly, laughing until they were side by side, wiping tears out of their eyes.

"Pretty good joke," I said.

Alex wrapped an arm around Dominica's neck and gave her a squeeze. "I love my sister," she said.

Dominica looked at Alex and said, "Me too."

"O. K. Great," I said, retaking my seat at the table. "That takes care of that. Everybody's happy. We got anything sweet for dessert?"

They grinned at each other for a second, and then, like girls in a water ballet, sprung their legs open wide.

IN THE MORNING I went for a paper from the rack outside the main entrance. Dominica and Dzubas were standing on the front stoop looking at a figure eight drawn in what looked like sand on the cement. It was raining steadily, but we were under the portico. I said, "It's nice. What is it?"

"Grits," Dzubas said.

"I'm sorry?"

"It's not sand," Dominica said. "It's grits. You know, grits. Food. Somebody did it in the middle of the night. It's a figure-eight."

I pushed at the edge of the eight with the toe of my shoe. The drawing was six feet long and three wide, an almost perfect symmetrical figure.

"Don't touch it," Dzubas said.

"It's voodoo," Dominica said.

"Come on," I said.

"It's true," Dzubas said. "I looked it up." He showed me a pocket book with a red-striped spider on the cover—*Layman's Guide to Black Magic.*

"Maybe it isn't Mel," Dominica said. "Maybe something's going on."

"That's a pretty thought," Dzubas said.

"No. I mean it's probably some prank, some kid."

Dzubas opened the door. "Hang on. Don't mess it up. I want to get a camera, take a picture."

Dominica looked out toward the highway at a black van that was passing. Without turning around she said, "It's got to be him."

Dzubas came back with the camera, one of those disk types that Kodak started making recently. He took his pictures and left, and then we got a broom and swept the grits into the parking lot.

Dominica said, "Big time in Odalisque, eh? And what was this stuff in the car on the way back? My car?"

"We were playing. She's like somebody I don't know, you know what I mean? I recognize her and everything, but something is missing, some connection we used to have. It's more than that, even. It's like she doesn't notice that this is missing, or doesn't admit she notices."

"She admitted it to me," Dominica said. "She hates it. She cried a lot last night."

"After the party," I said.

"Yes. She feels guilty. She hates herself for not feeling what she used to. She's sad. It isn't much fun being back there alone. She doesn't want to show you because you'll get the wrong idea."

"That'd be like me," I said.

"She'll be fine, talking and everything, and then suddenly her face cracks, like she's going to cry. It's awful. Painful. I wish you guys had never split up."

"Uh-huh," I said.

The lobby was a low-ceiling area that opened into the atrium behind us. We were facing the Gulf, watching the rain outside, watching the cars buzz by throwing sheets of water off to their sides. The thunder was constant and close and muffled. It shook the building. Bursts of air shot through the lobby and opened the outside doors an inch at a time. It seemed as if everything around us was moving. A flatbed truck lumbered by on the highway with a huge piece of industrial equipment strapped to its bed. The equipment was partially covered with a dark green tarp that was wet and flapping in the wind.

I hugged Dominica. She brought her arm up around my waist. There was a sun tan lotion scent in the air, the old kind of sun tan lotion, like Coppertone, or Sea & Ski. I sniffed, then leaned closer to her and sniffed at her shoulder, then her neck.

"What's wrong?" she said, spinning away from me. "What're you doing? I took a shower. Quit it."

"Smells good," I said.

"I never pressed him," she said. "I mean, if it isn't him I think I ought to do something, don't you?" She swung her hands out at her sides. "I don't know. Maybe I'm nuts. Do you want some pancakes? I want some pancakes."

"A great idea," I said. "You making?"

"I thought we'd get Alex and visit the not-to-be-believed Pancake House. Take an interest in the tenants, that sort of thing. You get Alex, O. K.? I'm going to change. I don't like these clothes. I'm going to put on something yellow."

Dzubas and Jane came with us. Jane made us promise that we wouldn't let her eat anything.

Turner was happy to see us. His franchise was done up in lemon vinyl and white trim, with big photographs of

cruise ships scattered around the walls. He had a few cus-
tomers, about a fifty-fifty mix of locals and tourists, but
half the place was empty. He saw us coming across the
parking lot and met us at the door. "You won't regret it,"
he said. "I'm going to stuff you with pancakes that'll
make your head spin."

"My idea of a good time," Dzubas said.

Turner led us to a round table by the front window,
then called for the waitress to come over and wipe the ta-
bletop. "Can't be too careful," he said, dishing out the
menus, which were typed and stapled to frying-pan-
shaped hunks of plywood. "Now. Some of this stuff I'm
still working on." He leaned over Dominica's shoulder
and pointed at the right edge of the menu. "This over
here is new, and I don't recommend it. Over here you got
your traditionals. Some of these peach guys in the fruit
group? They're O. K. Anything with a berry in it is O. K.
I don't know who put that bacon and egg job over there."
He took her menu and scratched something on it with a
ballpoint. Then he tore the menu sheet off the board and
gave Dominica a fresh menu. "I feel pretty good about
these combos, except the Burger'N'Bean. Forget that. I
can't figure that sucker out, know what I mean?"

The girl who had wiped the table was across the room
waiting on a young couple who appeared to be playing
tug of war with a baby, arguing about who the baby was
going to sit beside. The waitress settled that by bringing a
high chair, but then the couple started buttering a piece
of toast together—he held the toast, while she slapped on
the butter.

Turner was standing behind Dominica, gazing out at
the rain.

Jane said, "I want some of these MicroJacks. How many of those do you get?"

"Six," Turner said. "They're real good too. Light as little balloons. You won't believe it. They almost float away. You go to flip 'em and they kind of linger, you know? Up in the air. Good choice."

"Great," she said. "And orange juice. Big glass."

He nodded, scribbling the order on the back of the menu sheet he'd taken from Dominica. "Next?"

"What's this?" Dzubas said, reaching across the table to point to Dominica's menu.

"Those are like the size of fingers—they're our smallest," Turner said. "They come with a cream glaze and a pan steak. More of a supper thing, really."

"Ah," Dzubas said, nodding.

"The glaze is like a lotion you might put on," Turner said. "After you were burned or something. It's cool, cool-tasting." He made a sour face and shook his head at Dzubas.

It took us ten minutes to order, and it took Turner that long again to produce the pancakes, and then he was back to watch. He twisted his chair around and sat leaning on its back, smiling.

Dzubas said, "You know what I think's weird? Dwarfs. Frightening. They hate us, I guess."

"Don't be silly," Alex said.

"No, listen. When I was in Louisiana, in school—this was around Mardi Gras. So somehow I got to this place outside of New Orleans, like, in the woods. Big house with a gray painted porch. There were all these white wicker chairs with these striped cushions, and we sat out

there with these lime slices in our drinks—the lawn was
huge and it was black out there. Big old trees and marsh
grass and steam rising out of crawfish holes. Inside an old
black woman was preparing the dinner table with a white
cloth. I was out there with these two women I'd bumped
into in the Quarter, they were from somewhere, I don't
remember. They knew the people with the house. So,
anyway, except for them and me and the black woman,
all the rest of the people were dwarfs. I'm not kidding."

"So what happened?" Turner said. He had his chin on
his hands, his head about table-height.

"It was a party. But when we tried to leave, on the
bridge going back into town, we got in this car crash. It
wasn't our fault. A truck hit a Lincoln next to us. Guess
who was in the Lincoln?" He looked around the table as
if he knew we weren't going to guess. "Dwarfs," he said.
"A dozen of the ones from the house. It was crazy. This
old woman dwarf got her elbow all torn up. I went over
and looked at her, and the skin was torn away so you
could see muscles and stuff—like a medical illustration.
Anyway, she was all dressed up like a gypsy, or a wiz-
ard—spangles and jewelry and gold thread-patterns in her
dress. I blacked out. I woke up at a bait camp on edge of
the lake. The blond woman I was with was trying to
phone a hospital. I stopped her, and she took me back to
her motel, which was out in Slidell. But she wants me
to sleep in her car, a white Cadillac, because she says her
mother is in the room with her little sisters. Her mother is
Baptist, she tells me. This is nineteen sixty, sixty-one. So
we do all our business in the car for a while and then she
goes in and I stay in the Cadillac with the cracked-up

fender. When I get up the next day it's incredible out-side—the fog is so thick you can't see one end of the car from the other. I wipe off the window in the back seat there, and I can't see a thing. I don't know where I am. It's cold. I'm all bent up from sleeping in the car. So I get out and go up to the motel room door—this is one of those single-story places with individual units, so I figure she parked in front of her room, right? I knock on the door. It's about six a.m. or something, I guess, but I have to pee, so I knock again. So who comes to the door? This dwarf woman. Blonde."

"Dzubas," I said.

"No shit," he said, stabbing his pancakes a couple of times for emphasis. "I swear to God. I mean, I know it's not the woman I was with, but I'm confused, so I hold my hand up about shoulder height and I say, 'Where's, uh, . . .' and I realize I don't know the woman's name, the one I was with, but that doesn't seem to matter. She lets me in and the room is wall-to-wall dwarfs. They're all asleep. There's maybe fifty people in this room with imi-tation wood paneling, the cream-colored kind, and these small people are all over the beds, on the floor, on the couch, the dresser—everywhere."

"No girl, right?" Turner said. He nodded as if he un-derstood.

"Wrong," Dzubas said. "She was right in the middle of it, spread-eagled on the bed with hairy little naked guys stuck all over her. I'm not joking. I stood there a minute, staring at her, then I backed out and got sick in the flow-erbed."

Turner jumped off his chair and clapped his hands to-gether. "You liked her, right? That's great."

"Seems kind of pointless to me," Jane said. "So she liked dwarfs, so what?"

"So he thinks they're weird," Dominica said.

"I was thinking about all this voodoo stuff and I remembered her," Dzubas said. "Sorry."

"Voodoo?" Alex said.

"Listen," Turner said. "How about these hotcakes?"

"Dwarf voodoo," Jane said.

"He didn't tell you about the eight?" Dominica said to Alex.

"Somebody drew a big eight on the doorstep last night. Dzubas read about it in his voodoo book—a warning to devotees of the evil lurking within. Me, I gather."

"Next you get frog intestines in the mail," Jane said. "Guaranteed to make you puke."

"The hotcakes were perfect, Rob," Alex said. "Really."

"Oh," he said. "Thanks."


THE RAIN hadn't quit, but it had slacked off, and Alex wanted to take a walk after breakfast, so we took one umbrella and left the group at the Pancake House, walking up the highway toward SeaSide. She had on a big coat and black galoshes, and she looked worn out. "I got drunk last night," she said when we were a couple hundred yards along the road. "I don't like getting drunk. I hate it. Especially wine." She stopped and brushed her hair away from her face, lifted the hair up and back over her shoulders, then let it fall in wet curls around the collar of the coat. "Never mind. I don't know what I'm doing here. I shouldn't have come."

"It's fine, it's good," I said. "I'm glad you came."

"I'll bet. I'm just the tiger you wanted to see, right? Anyway, I've been thinking about you. At home. I've been seeing this kid from the office, and every time he comes over I wish he was you."

I made a noise through my teeth and smiled at her.

"Well, not you, but like you," she said. "He's nice and everything, but he's mole-ish. Part of it is that he's small. I've always hated small men. When I'm with a small man everything shrinks. I feel like I'm in a small town having a little life washing tiny red pants. Shorts. Buttons up and down the fly. You get the idea: small apartment, small yard—I hang the pants on the line in the dreary after-noon sunlight. It's not great."

I reached out to touch her. She didn't react. She let me run my knuckles along the edge of her ear, then down the line of her chin. I put my arm around her and we walked a while on the water-splashed highway, like old lovers.

Then she said, "What about you? You get hooked up with my sister." She shook her head and pulled away from me. "Boy, I hate that."

"I'm not exactly hooked up," I said. "I don't know what I'm doing any more than you do. I came down here and . . ."

"Spare me the details, will you?"

"I was trying to say . . ."

She patted my arm. "I know what you're trying. But you don't need to help me. Maybe my next one will be Spiderman or somebody. I just wish you had a brother. A good brother."

"You want me to call my mom and tell her to get after it?"

"I see," she said. "Keep me clean a minimum of sixteen years, that it? Not to mention the other minor flaws in the concept."

"Caught me," I said. "I admit it."

"Don't worry," she said. "It's much more fevered and exciting in imagination than it is in real life."

"Same here," I said.

"Watch it. That's my sister you're talking about."

She linked her arm in mine and pulled me close again, wrapping her other arm across my chest, leaning her head into my shoulder. We didn't talk for a while. The Gulf shined like mylar, reflecting the seamless slate gray of the sky. Spines ran out from the shore into the flat water, their dark posts erect like soldiers marching, shortest first. The water looked soft. A few trees in back of the scrub line were bent and isolated like women with tired backs, arched over the darkened sand. We listened to the rapid tap of the rain, the scrapes of barrels under piers, the sighs of heavy cables going taut, then slack, and the enveloping white noise of the sea wind. Our footsteps sloshing through the shallow depressions in the blacktop. In a few minutes we came to SeaSide. It looked desolate, its panels of sherbet colors paler than usual in the gray light, glass the color of Coke bottles, white aluminum. Across the highway the restaurant, jacked up on tall pilings, sat like an experiment in weather. The bird sign was on, bright and brittle against the muggy sky. We stopped and watched the suddenly red bird lift its wings in jerky steps, then close them again, over and over.

At eleven that night Alex and I were sitting at a white enameled table by the pool watching Dominica play Hana Fuda with Jane, who was losing gracefully. Dzubas had just come out of the water. He was standing beside Jane, drying himself with a beach towel. None of the other guests were around. There was a lot of noise outside, then somebody who looked like a refugee from *The Road Warrior* yanked open the pool door and rode a beat-up motorcycle into the atrium. The rider wore a black helmet painted to look like slicked-back hair, boots with chrome chains around them, and torn leather pants and jacket. The pants were tight, full of big zippers. Both rider and motorcycle were spattered with mud and dust. When he parked the bike he stayed on it for a minute, sitting side-saddle, watching us look at him. Finally, he lifted the black visor and grinned. "Howdy," he said. He got up and wrestled the helmet off, then pushed at his matted hair with a gloved hand. "How we doing?" he said.

We all said O. K. at once, so it sounded more foolish than it had to. Dominica was the first to recover. "Hello, Melvin. What're you supposed to be?"

"Queen?" he said, swaggering toward us. He propped one of his boots on the brick planter by our table and pulled his jacket open from the neck to the middle of his chest. He wasn't wearing a shirt. There was a large black spider with two red dots on its back tattooed at the base of Mel's neck. "Martin and Alex," he said. "How've you been?"

"I've been moderate," Alex said.

"Me too," I said. "Maybe less moderate than my friend."

"That's the truth," Alex said.

"So this is Mel," Jane said. She got up and circled him as if sizing him up. "I'm Jane. You look pretty rugged for an insurance guy."

"Gave it up," he said. "Too many dead people in insurance, so I got out. I'm a hundred percent real estate."

"O. K.," Dominica said, picking up the cards and stacking them in piles.

"I thought maybe I'd roll on down here and be friendly," Mel said, reaching toward her head. "Didn't you used to have hair up here somewhere?"

She dodged his hand, then started to put the cards in her pocket. "Went away," she said.

"This the Nip game you always liked? What's it called? Hana Fuda, right? I spent a long time playing this game." He took the cards out of her hand and looked at them, one at a time. Then he dropped the deck on the table, scattering the cards. "Oops," he said, stumbling forward to get the cards. "Sorry."

Dominica said, "You ready to lose the costume? Take a bath? I'll set up a room." She left the table, going around the end of the pool toward her apartment.

"I guess I'm not sleeping with her tonight," Mel said, shrugging at the rest of us.

"Or any other night," she said over her shoulder. "And get the motorcycle out, O. K.?"

He stared after her, waiting until she was inside, then said, "Welcome home, Mel. You look tired, Mel. You need a holiday, Mel."

"Did you do the eight?" Dzubas said.

Mel looked us over before he answered. "Uh, I don't think so," he finally said. "What is it? You mean an eight eight?" He drew a figure eight in the air.

"Yep," Dzubas said. "Somebody painted an eight on the doorstep last night."

"I was in New Orleans," Mel said. He rattled his chains and smiled at us. "Whatever it is, I didn't do it. My brother Minnie is coming tomorrow. He can testify on my behalf—oh, I get it. It's Dominica's ex-husband routine, right? The driving-her-crazy version?"

There was an awkward silence at the table. It hadn't occurred to me that he might not be involved at all, or that the whole thing might be a routine. I said, "There's this strange stuff going on. The eight is only part of it."

"Always was," Mel said. "The autopsy, right? Small fires mysteriously lit? Dolls in the refrigerator? So you figure it's a plan to eliminate the ex-wife? Well, sure, I've been working on that. I think a mortar's a good way to go, don't you? Simple, quick. Loud. A clean wound." He slapped Dzubas on the back. "But first I've got to take the motorcycle outside. Doctor's orders."

We watched him straddle the bike and walk it back to the door. When he was gone I said, "I see."

Dzubas shrugged, spreading his hands in front of him. "He doesn't seem the evil genius type, does he?"

"I thought you knew him," I said.

"I met him a couple of times, but it was long time ago. We said hello and I left. I mean, what do you expect him to say, that he did it?"

"You asked the question," Jane said.

"My up-the-gut strategy," Dzubas said. "You know,

direct assault on the subject. I saw Charles Bronson do it once."

"No doubt," Jane said.

"This is Mel?" Alex said, shuffling her hand toward where Mel had been and looking at me. "Was he like this when he came to see us?"

I shook my head. "He was a sweetheart when he came to see us, but he was heartbroken, remember?"

Jane looked at her nails. "He's not what I expected. I pictured a business suit guy with an attaché in Cordovan leather. Clean and prissy. But he comes in a cross between Lou Albano and Mr. Happy."

I flicked a ladybug off an elephant ear leaf that stuck out of the planter and hung over the chair next to mine.

"If it's not Mel doing the crazy stuff I think we ought to hit the road in a major way," Dzubas said.

"An endearing aspect of our friend and co-resident," Jane said. "World record holder in the cut-and-run."

THE LIVING ROOM windows in Alex's apartment faced away from the Gulf, toward the wooded property behind the motel where the plane sat in among the trees. I'd been in her place five minutes when I saw the lights out by the plane go on. "Look at this," I said, calling Alex to the window. "I wonder if I should go out there?"

"Let her alone," she said. "Sit down. Eat your snack."

My snack was a fried chicken breast she'd bought earlier at the Mini-Mart a couple hundred yards back up the highway. In her refrigerator there were three of these, each on a piece of white bread, the two wrapped together with clear plastic. The guy at the Mini-Mart had dozens of them.

"I'm taking off tomorrow," Alex said. "I told Dominica. She wanted me to stay around."

"You should stay. Especially now."

"Don't tell me what I should do, O. K.? I'll talk to Mel. It sounded as if he knew about the crazy stuff—did she show you the postcard? It was horrible."

I watched the plane and ate my chicken. Alex sat on the couch beside me—it was a cowboy couch with a rustic wood frame stained dark, tan cushions with red piping, a lasso-and-cow-skull design embroidered in the center of the back. When I finished the chicken she picked up the plate and the crumpled paper napkin and went to the kitchen.

I said, "I think I ought to be sure she's all right."

"So go," Alex said, bending so she could see me through the window-like opening between the kitchen and living room. "Get over there and root hog or die. I'm not stopping you."

"Take it easy," I said. "Maybe they're out here." I went to the front door and looked out. Mel was sitting on the end of the diving board, staring down at the water. There wasn't anybody else in the atrium. He didn't see me. I shut the door quietly. "Mel's out here swimming," I said, crowding into the tiny kitchen. "I guess that means she's O. K."

Alex was washing dishes. She had one sink full of suds, and water running in the other. "I'll tell you what," she said. "You find Dominica. I'll go to bed."

"O. K.," I said. "I'll go to bed too."

I wrapped my arms around her waist. She pulled them away, one by one, with soapy hands. "No, thanks," she said.

"Right," I said. I went back to the window and looked at the plane. The lights were still on. I was tired. All of a sudden I felt as though I could sleep for a week. While I was watching, the lights in the plane snapped off and I couldn't see anythng out there except the silhouette of the trees against the sky. I felt sick to my stomach. I wished it was still raining and Dominica was in the apartment with me, and Alex out in the plane. I wished Dominica had been Alex in the first place, years ago. I thought about being seventeen. When I was seventeen my girlfriend invited me to go to Corpus Christi with her and her family for a weekend. I couldn't go, I don't remember why. I was horribly in love with this girl, who was blond, tall, shy, naive. It was the first time I'd been in love. Maybe not the first, but it felt as if it were. This girl was nice the way only young girls can be, the way that puts your heart in your throat every moment you're with her, the way that makes every raindrop a thing of terrifying beauty. We were together on many rainy nights, walking branch-littered suburban streets with our pants rolled up, and on other, colder nights we warmed each other's hands, faces, lips. We sat in heated car interiors on deserted roads out in the country, watching the clear, bright sky, waiting for the weather to make us cold enough so we had to start the engine again. The heater smell was delicious, like some burning chemical, bitter and pungent. I remembered the look of headlights spiralling down an empty two-lane road cloaked by trees and an occasional low house with dim lights in its windows, and the dull glow on the horizon in the distance, where the city was. The girl's laughter was as delicate and frail as new ice. Now I wanted her breath on the side of my face, on my cheek, at the edge of my mouth, wanted to stop with her in my mother's Chevrolet on a wooden plank bridge over a tiny creek somewhere, wanted to watch the mirror for signs of coming cars, listen for the sound of an engine over the smooth, fabric-like ripple of the dark water below us, while she reached for me, kissed the side of my face nearest her, kissed tenderly, but with the urgency of a young girl hoping to please, with soft dry lips alongside my eye, wanted her to get to her knees on the squealing vinyl seat so that she could rub her lips over mine, wedge herself between me and the steering wheel—I wanted that night on the bridge, in the car filled with sweet air, wet jasmine, honeysuckle.

Alex startled me, slipping her arms around my waist and flattening her cheek against my back. I jumped, then turned my head. The apartment was dark. "Sorry," she said, standing behind me, looking over my shoulder at the dark yard, at the silhouetted trees, at the spot where the airplane sat in the woods. "We aren't the ones, are we?" she said.

I patted the backs of her hands, then gently separated them and stepped out of her grip.

MINNIE ARRIVED at ten the next morning in a pickup with a giant statue of a horse in the bed. I was by the pool with Dzubas and Jane. I hadn't seen Dominica, and Alex

was off for a walk with Mel, who looked much more ordinary in daylight and without his motorcycle gear.

Minnie was short. His Hawaiian shirt didn't fit and his
khakis were too long by about six inches. His shoes were
busting open at the laces and there was a chicken-liver
sized bump on his head, near the crown, clearly visible
through the few strands of light-colored hair which grew
there. He climbed out of the truck and loped up to where
we were sitting and introduced himself. "Hi," he said.
"I'm Minnie. Mel's brother, Minnie. Who're you?"

"I'm Martin," I said. "That's Jane. This is Dzubas."

"Wow," Minnie said. "What a name. I like it. And
look at that arm. How'd that happen? You always have
that, or did you have an accident?"

"Broke it," Dzubas said.

"I see, I see," Minnie said. He turned and waved toward the truck. "I brought the horse. Like him? He's actual size. I've been here before, you know. I like it here."

"Mel's out at the beach," I said.

"That's fine," he said. "That's good. Between you and
me—I mean I don't really want him to hear me say
this—but between you and me I'm not sure I'm going to
stay long, even though I like it here. I'm just carrying the
horse over, kind of a favor, you know?"

"I think I'll go find Mel," Jane said. She got up and
started across the pool apron.

"Oh, don't do that," Minnie said. "Not for me. I can
find him. I know my way around." He scanned the beach,
then sat down in one of the redwood chairs. "I may just
wait for him," he said. "My name's not really Minnie,
you know. Really it's John. But Mel's called me that ever

since I can remember, since time began. I think it's for Minnie Mouse or somebody like that. I don't mind. You know, I could really eat a banana right about now. A couple of bananas."

"I haven't seen a banana for weeks," Dzubas said.

"Maybe they've got some over at the Mini-Mart," Jane said.

"A Mini-Mart? Wow, what a great idea," Minnie said. He jumped up and looked in the direction Jane had pointed. "I don't see it," he said. "I see a gas station and a Tastee Freeze—that looks closed. Where is this Mini-Mart, anyway?"

Jane wrapped an arm around his shoulder. "Stick with me," she said. "I'll get you there."

"Terrific," he said, turning to me, then to Dzubas. "You guys want to come, too? We'll make it a party. I'm getting some chocolate milk and a couple of bananas, just for starters. Maybe some red suckers."

The four of us went to the Mini-Mart, cutting across the parking lot and then the empty field next to SeaSide. Minnie talked about his drive. "I was afraid to go too fast with horse back there. You never know, hit a bump and the guy might just fly outta there—am I spitting?" He was talking to Dzubas. "Am I spitting on you as I talk here? Sometimes I do that. I don't know it when I'm doing it, I mean, sometimes I see little trails zipping away, out of the corners of my eyes—not coming out of my eyes, but I see 'em with my eyes, see what I mean? But I don't really know."

Dzubas shook his head for no, then gave me a look behind Minnie's back.

Minnie got a cowboy handkerchief out of his back pocket. "It's very embarrassing if I am." He wiped his mouth, then held the handkerchief out in front of him. "Funny thing, isn't it? Handkerchief? I like it. It's a good idea. Anyway," he said, stuffing the handkerchief back in his pocket, "there I was on the highway coming through Mobile, and I hit this board that was in the road, you know? Well I thought I was a goner, I really did. Thought that horse was gonna dive in the bay. But it worked out. He just galloped around back there, then he settled down rock steady. Other than that it was fine. It was really O. K."

"Where'd you get it?" Jane said.

"I didn't get it," he said. "He got it. Got it in New Orleans, I believe. Was a sign of some kind, some kind of store. Probably a horse store, or something. Or maybe California—they make a lot of actual-size stuff in California. I've been there. I know it's true. I like the actual-size trees they make out there."

There weren't any bananas at the Mini-Mart, so Minnie bought himself a box of lemon-filled doughnuts and a pint of Scientific brand chocolate milk. He also bought a four-foot inflatable rhinoceros float, the last one they had. "I've always wanted one of these," he said. "This one's kind of small, though. It's probably a baby or something."

The rest of us got soft drinks, and then we all crossed the highway to the beach to wait for Mel and Alex. We went down to the water's edge and found a place to sit. Minnie seemed preoccupied with keeping the sand off his food first, then his clothes. He sat on the rhino, which, because it had been on display at the store, was already about half-inflated. He passed the box of doughnuts. Jane and I split one.

"So let's see," Minnie said, brushing and straightening his pantsleg. "What's the story down here? How's Miss Dominica? She doing all right? I really like her, I really do. She's about O. K. with Minnie. Mel should just give her this place and then maybe she'd like him again. He's crazy if he doesn't like her, according to me. No lie."

"I thought she got it in the divorce," Dzubas said. "That's what I heard."

Minnie made a face and shook his head. "No sir. She didn't get anything to speak of. I told him it was a terrible thing, but did he listen to me? No sir. Never does. I said to him, I said, Hey, be a nice guy for a change, how about? Really. Didn't work. She got some kind of arrangement—they own it together, I think that's what it is. That's as far as the judge was gonna go. I said it was wrong." He flipped his shirt to get some sand off, then stared up the beach. "What happened to the sun?" he said. "What is this, monsoon season?"

"This year," Jane said.

"It's all right," he said. "I like rain. Brings out the salamanders. I like to catch 'em and wear 'em on my ears. I used to do it when I was a kid. Still do. No difference, except maybe they don't hang down so far any more. I think they're littler than they used to be, you know? Maybe we're having some kind of salamander crisis."

"Hello, Minnie." Mel had come up behind us, without us hearing.

Minnie jumped up and hugged him. "Hiya, Boss. I got

the horse. You see the horse? Looks good. Looks like a million."

"I saw it," Mel said. The spider tattoo, I noticed, had faded a lot since the night before. It must've been done with a felt-tip pen.

"Had a couple of tough spots on the way over," Minnie said. "But the rest was take it easy, greasy, you got a long way to slide—remember that? You want a lemon doughnut?"

Mel took a doughnut and took a tiny bite out of its edge.

Minnie said, "I've been talking to these folks." He slapped Dzubas on the shoulder. "Isn't that a great name, Dzubas? I like it. We've been talking about life and stuff. What about you? You been walking?"

"Uh-huh," Mel said, nibbling at his doughnut.

The tide had exposed a sand bar where some fish were flipping around, trying to find the water. Minnie said, "Look at that."

Jane splashed out to the bar and tossed the fish into deeper water. "Mullet," she said, coming back toward us.

Minnie was clapping. "Good work," he said. "Got to look after 'em sometimes, and they'll look after you. Right, Mel? That's the kind of thing Mel's always telling me. If it isn't fish, it's something else—dogs, horses." He picked up his rhino float. "See this guy, Mel? I got him over at the store there? Last one." He primped the float as if he were working on a show dog for a key judge. "It's pretty good, isn't it? You got a pump around here? We're going to have to go electric on a guy this size."

"There's one in the laundry room," Dzubas said.

"Tiny one." He held out his hands as if holding a basket-ball. "It's slow, but it works."

"Well," Minnie said. "O. K. Good. I'm going to go fill him up and take a look. He's kind of bad-looking since I've been sitting on him."

"I'll go with you," Mel said. He turned to me and Dzubas. "We can use a hand later getting the horse down, O. K.? First I've got to find out where she wants it. Sometime after lunch?"

We said we'd help. Mel and Minnie went off across the beach together. The three of us stayed where we were and watched them go. Finally, Dzubas said, "I'm about due for a vacation. Maybe a trip to Chicago. Am I spitting on you guys?"

"Not nice," Jane said. "I think somebody better talk to Dominica."

"That's my thinking," Dzubas said, smoothing a fan shape in the sand with his cast. "But what will somebody say?"

I looked over toward the motel. Mel and Minnie were beside the truck, admiring the horse.


DOMINICA WAS ALONE in the plane. She looked like she hadn't slept. There were dark patches around her eyes, her clothes were sloppy, her hands were constantly at her mouth, rubbing at her lips, pinching them. She kept swiveling her head as if she were trying to find a comfortable position for it, but couldn't. I stood on the platform outside and she stayed inside, and we watched a pelican flying low over the water, left to right, watched it drop as if it had suddenly forgotten how to fly, and splash awkwardly in the water, then float a few seconds before taking off again, continuing its trip. "He's late," she finally said.

"Bad day," I said.

She smiled at that and stepped back from the hatch so I could climb inside. "Don't look at me," she said. "Wait a minute." She went to the bed, stripped off her clothes and dropped them on the floor, picked a white silk robe off the back of a chair. "I'm going to wash my face now," she said, tying the robe's belt at her waist.

When she came out of the tiny bath she looked better. I said, "New woman."

She sat on the bed and pressed the robe between her legs. "Just before we came here I was in Miami," she said, staring at her forearms. "I fell in love with the guy who played the organ in the music shop at the Regional Mall. He wasn't attractive. He was plain—pasty and fat. I stood at the window watching him play, watching his back roll slowly with the music. His shirt was wretched, white-on-white. I felt something when I saw him, as if he knew something special, as if he did not mind being put on display in that window, his back to passersby, because he was satisfied, complete. He could handle the indignity. There was a pleat at the back of his shirt, and, as he played, the pleat opened and closed like an accordion. He played mostly Spanish music, standards, and his playing lacked any sort of touch. I mean, it was skating music. At noon he left the store and I followed him to the lunch counter at the far end of the mall. It was one of those places with cherry drinks spraying inside big plastic dispensers. I sat opposite him and for the first time I saw his eyes, which were an extraordinary blue, like blue neon. He knew I'd followed him. He ordered a sandwich and I ordered a lemonade. I caught his eye again and I stared at him, held his gaze for nearly a minute. That was it. He left shortly after that. I stayed at the counter, nursing the lemonade. Later, about six, I waited for him ouside the music store. We left together without saying a word. We went in his car to a motel downtown. He told me his name was Hobart. I undressed him. His skin was stretchy and white, dotted with long black hairs. I made love to him. I did every slutty thing I could think of, things I'd seen in magazines and movies, things I'd heard about, things I imagined would be filthy—everything. The whole time he barely moved, he sat there on his fat white butt and took it. A couple of hours later I left him fifty dollars and walked away."

I waited a few minutes after she'd finished, then said, "You're a terrible person."

"No. That's not what I'm thinking. I'm thinking I want to do it again."

"Well," I said, slapping my hands together. "It's good luck I dropped by."

She smiled and pulled my arm into her lap, stroking it the way she might a puppy. "Will you stop?"

"Sorry," I said.

"I guess you got the corrected information?" She gave me a sheepish look. "I own half. The snake picture he did when we were fighting. It's from this thing I was telling you. The grits I honestly don't know about. I mean, I'm not scared, but I didn't do it either. Toole I don't know about. Maybe he works for Isabel. The rest is true. I mean, about Mel. He was a pain after the divorce. He was expressing his anger, I think." She sighed. "That's it. I want you to stay around."

She ran her fingers down my arm. Near my wrist her hand jerked as if scorched. The spasm shot through her, shaking her shoulders in the silk robe, opening its neck, and then she got control, and the fingers went smoothly again. "Fear of rejection," she said.

I kissed her temple. "Not likely," I said.

She got up and went to the wardrobe that was poised awkwardly on one side of the cabin, propped up on pocket books. "The boy likes me," she said. "Maybe I'll show him some of my dresses." She turned around. "I look sexy in dresses. Want to see some?"

"I don't think that's necessary. You're doing O. K. in the robe."

"I've always loved it," she said, untying and then retying the belt. "I guess it is kind of swank, isn't it?"

I said it was and watched her move around the small cabin. She was showing off, up on her toes, lovely—the cords in her throat, the shadows of her collarbone, the little traces of thigh that cut through when the robe opened slightly. She wasn't penitent or sad now, she was loose, elegant—wanting me to watch her, wanting to show herself to me. She came my way, so I started up off the bed, but she just kissed my cheek and gave me a soft push, then moved to the other side of the table and leaned over the tape player sorting through her cassettes. The robe came open at the neck. "Stay where you are," she said, smiling at me as she slid a tape into the player and started the music. "I'm doing this one."

• • •

ALEX SAID she knew where I'd been. "I didn't come after you with a bat. So I'm proud of myself." It was afternoon and the rain had returned. Thunder cracked and rolled across the dark sky. We were in the atrium, waiting for Mel and Dominica and Minnie, who were getting planks so we could slide the horse out of the truck. She drew a couple of stick figures in the condensation on the glass. "I'm not happy about you and little sister. I mean, I hate it. You weren't interested in her before, were you? How could you be, you only met her once. You weren't interested in her, but you thought she was pretty. I remember you told me that. You said she was sexy."

"Everybody's sexy these days."

"Some more than others," she said. She drew a knife on the glass, its tip sticking through one of the figures. "This is you," she said, tapping the glass. "I'm up here with the knife." She used her fist to wipe out the drawing, then held me in an awkward, cool embrace. "Mel thinks she's got problems. He said he wasn't doing anything. He did a couple of things a long time ago, but not recently."

"She told me," I said.

"I think he's overreacting. He's kind of nuts."

"We just call him Spider," I said.

"I saw that. It's not so strange. You used to do lightning bolts on me with a Pentel. On my tits, remember?"

"In the privacy of our own home," I said.

"I think maybe we were a little too private," she said. "I hate this. Can we stop?"

We stopped. We stood there side by side and looked at

the water coming down the glass and waited until Dominica called to us that Minnie and Mel were already outside. Then I went out to help them get the horse down. What was interesting about the horse was how crummy it was when you got close to it. It wasn't a horse anybody would want to own.

"We're thinking about the beach," Mel said, pointing across the highway. "Somewhere out there."

"We're thinking about an in-the-middle-of-nowhere thing," Minnie said. "It's right for me." He made a director's rectangle with his thumbs and first fingers, and looked across at the beach. "I can see it out there, all alone, standing there."

"Displaying human emotions and aspirations," I said.

"He doesn't like it," Mel said, jerking his thumb to one side. "Take it back."

It took us an hour to get the horse where he wanted it on the beach. Afterwards, Mel said we should get a beer to celebrate. Minnie said he hated beer. I said I wanted to change, but Mel insisted, so we left Minnie and took the truck into town. We stopped at a tavern called Lou-Lou's Top Hat, but it was closed, so we went across the street to the grocery. He went in to get the beer. When he came back we sat in the truck, in the parking lot, facing the store's entrance. "Divorce," he said, raising his bottle.

"Second thoughts," I said. I tilted my bottle at the window of the grocery, then took a swallow.

"I don't have much to say," he said. "I'm not guilty. But she told you that, right?"

"Yep," I said. I was staring at a hand-painted squash on a sign in the window. The squash had a smile painted on it in red.

"She can be lovely," he said. "You have to be careful, though. She operates in strange ways—listen, this is stupid." He turned around in the seat to look at me. "I'm worried about her."

"Worried about what?"

He faced forward again. "She gets depressed. Talks about killing herself. I never could deal with it."

"Alex thinks she's O. K.," I said.

"Maybe," he said. "She doesn't like me coming around. When we get out of here, maybe it'll be O. K. I'm taking Minnie down to Key West. He always wanted to see it. We're going tomorrow, probably."

I nodded. He tapped the beer bottle against the steering wheel. We sat in silence for a minute. Then he said, "She scares me. That's why I divorced her. She didn't want it. She said it was O. K. if I wanted to just leave. I filed anyway. I had to."

I said, "You and Alex. She told me the same thing, only it was the other way around. I mean, I wanted to move out without doing anything legal. She said she couldn't do that. I don't know what difference it makes."

"She didn't want to get married. I did. My father always said leave things the way you find them."

"So did mine," I said.

"It was a big idea at one time," he said. "My father had plenty of big ideas. Our house had copper walls—covered with sheet copper. We had rolls and rolls of it. We wrapped the house with this copper, hammered it, sprayed it with acid because that was supposed to turn it blue. Only we used the wrong acid and the copper didn't change much. Inside we had Bauhaus furniture on the corners of a thirty-foot homemade rug he'd patterned after a Coptic textile he'd seen in a liquor ad. Outside we had long throws of thick grass, a gravel drive, a high brick wall, and prairie. No neighbors for five hundred yards in any direction."

"Where was this?"

"Texas," Mel said. "My father told me that when his father was dying they called him into the hospital room. His father was naked on a gurney. A small nurse, an Irish woman, told him to hold his father's penis. She said, 'No matter what happens, you hang onto this. We're working up here, and you hold it so it points at that window over there.' The place was filled with doctors and nurses clustered around his father's head and chest. His father was still alive, but failing fast. My father was still a boy, you see? He didn't know what he was doing, but he thought it might help, because why else would the nurse tell him to do it? He told me the penis was small and red, like a dog's penis, and it was wet when he took hold of it."

"This is a true story?" I said.

"That's what he said. He was there maybe twenty minutes, and then his father finally started to pee, and it kept coming out, all over the place, an endless stream of pee, splashing all over my father, the old man's legs, the gurney, the room, and his father was crapping too, so there was a stink in the room, but the doctors and nurses were high and dry. When it was over the Irish nurse gave him a towel."

Mel held up his hand as if to examine his palm. The hand was ten inches from his face. He let it close into a loose fist. "His idea of a lesson, I think. Or maybe it was too ugly to keep secret. He knew the power of a secret."

I grunted. Then I leaned forward and stood my empty bottle on the dash. The rain was fizzing up at the curb in front of us. I was ready to go back to the motel and change my clothes. I said, "You ready to head back?"

"Sure," he said, starting the truck's engine. "I need to get straightened away for tomorrow." He pulled a sheet of ruled paper out of his pocket. The paper was wet. "Here's where we are in Key West. If you need me."

ALEX WAS in my apartment when I got back. She was wearing a wrinkled gauze dress, plum colored and open low in front, over a white Danskin that had tiny triangles all over it. Her hair was up, and she had on heels. She looked too elegant for the setting, as if she were going somewhere. I asked if she was.

"I got cleaned up," she said. "That's all. I did call the airline. Made reservations and everything. I don't think it's healthy for me around here. Oh, and the horse fell over."

I went to the window to see.

"No," she said. "We got it back up. All of us pitched in. It was great in the rain. Minnie supervised, so it took time, but we got it done. He and Turner got along like gangbusters."

I said, "Will you excuse me for a minute while I change these clothes? I've been sitting in a truck soaking wet for the last hour."

"The new modesty." She followed me into the bedroom. "I'll watch. I like to watch men dress."

I stopped in the bathroom doorway and made a face at

her, then stripped, got a fresh towel, and started to dry
off. She lit a cigarette, which was unusual since she wasn't
a smoker, and watched me. "Dominica says I'm doing
the same thing to her that I accuse her of doing to me. I
told her I wasn't. I said I didn't want you back." She
tried, unsuccessfully, to blow a couple of smoke rings.

"That's flattering," I said.

"She says you're interesting in bed—that's her word. I
thought you'd like to know that. I said I knew." Alex
pinched the cigarette between her thumb and second finger, carried it into the bathroom, and flushed it down the
toilet. Coming back she slipped her palm across my bare
ass. "Cold," she said.

"You would be too," I said, stepping away from her.
"What else did she say?"

"She thinks she's more your speed. She's very involved
with people's speeds. Her personal opinion is that I
shouldn't have gone ahead with the divorce."

"She isn't alone." I pointed into the bathroom. "I'm
going in here, now. You coming?"

She shook her head. "I'll go help Dominica. She's having a big dinner tonight. Speeches and everything. I'm
doing the beets."

"I just love beets," I said. "Punch the lock on your way
out, will you? I may take a nap."

When she was gone I took off the jeans I'd put on too
hastily, and ran the bath water. I was stepping into the
tub when the phone rang. It was Dominica. I told her I
was going to take a hot bath.

"Oh," Dominica said. "I guess I'll just sit tight, then.
You feeling all right?"

"Great," I said. "We're having a dinner?"

"Mel and Minnie are taking off early tomorrow. It was Alex's idea. She doesn't want us disappearing. It hurts her."

"I know," I said. "But she can handle it."

"I don't like to hurt her," Dominica said. "We talked this afternoon. I miss her—you know, being with her sometimes. I stay over here and I forget about her. I've been thinking about a lot of stuff. I don't know—I'll tell you about it."

"Tell me what?"

"You know, what we talked about. It's not anything final or anything. Just ideas. Plans . . . Oh! She's here." Dominica said something away from the mouthpiece, to Alex, then said to me, "I'd better go now. Come over when you're ready. O. K.?"

I said I would, and hung up. Then I got in the tub.


DOMINICA AND Alex decided they didn't want to cook, so dinner was rescheduled for an oyster bar in Odalisque. We went in two cars—Alex, Dzubas, Turner, and me in the rental car, Dominica, Mel, Minnie, and Jane in the Mercedes. Turner tried to ride with them, but they sent him back to us.

Alex drove. I was in front with her. The rain had moved off to the west, but the highway was still damp, and it looked as if there was more rain behind us. Dzubas or Turner had gone heavy on the aftershave. A sweet-smelling, flowery scent filled the car. I cranked the window down to let some of it out. Nobody talked. We followed the Mercedes and I stared at the stumpy poles and the silver cables that wrapped every curve. Dominica took a different road than the one Alex and I had taken. It was a two-lane that had been widened into three lanes by moving the stripes around, and it went through Lullaby and several other towns, which were filled with honky-tonks and billboards. Fifteen minutes into the trip the Mercedes slowed and then peeled off into a parking lot in front of a roadside fruit stand. We pulled in beside the others.

"I'm getting some pears," Dominica said. She held onto my door and squatted so she could see Alex. "Anybody in here like pears?"

"Me," Alex said. She pushed open her door and got out, walking uncomfortably across the oyster-shell lot.

"Me too," Turner said, getting out. But he didn't go in. He went over to the Mercedes to talk to Minnie.

I sat in my seat and looked at the panels of afternoon light on the Avis car's dash. I was thinking of the picture with the snake face. I was trying to imagine it without the snake, trying to see Dominica with thick, glossy hair tumbling around her shoulders.

Dzubas leaned forward, resting his arms on the back of the front seat. "When I was teaching English I had this girl, a beautiful Italian girl, a senior. She was tall, with light skin and a few tiny flat moles, large eyes, storybook legs—she was perfect sex. She wrote every paper about her family. If you talked to her you'd think she was simple-minded, but she wrote these papers. One was about throwing chicken wings on the grave of her father, about

getting dressed up in a pretty church dress but not wearing anything underneath, and then sneaking out to the
cemetery in the middle of the night. It was a windy night.
The place was run down and scary—there were these
knob-like blue lights around to mark the paths, but most
of them were burned out or broken. She took a galvanized
bucket of chicken she'd baked and sat in the weeds next
to his plot lobbing these wings, one by one, on his grave."
He stopped, then slid back in his seat. "I could barely
keep my hands off her. It was horrible."

"Probably shouldn't have," I said. "Kept your hands
off her, I mean."

"The day after graduation she married a kid who managed a record store. I couldn't believe it. I wanted to run
after her and tell her to think again. I had this picture of
myself racing along the street surrounded by cans that his
pals had tied to the back of his Z-28, or whatever. Jesus. I
knew I'd never make it teaching."

Dominica and Alex were fooling around in the fruit
stand. Alex held a green banana on top of her head, like a
horn, and Dominica put lemons in her eye sockets—she
buzzed around a little, wobbling her fingers as if they
were feelers.

"You've got a problem there," Dzubas said from the
back seat. He tapped my shoulder and pointed at the sisters.

"Thanks for helping me out," I said.

They came out of the stand and swapped some fruit in
front of the car, then Alex got in and handed me a bag.
"Got pears, bananas, plums—where's Turner?"

"Visiting," I said. I looked at the other car. Turner was

climbing into the back seat. "For the duration, it appears."

The late afternoon sky was close, the clouds were like spills of dark Cool Whip going in slow motion across the sky. The road stretched out ahead of us, bordered on both sides by flat, empty fields. There wasn't any sun left. In a minute we passed an abandoned airport—diagonal slits of concrete shooting into the field, a maze of stubby landing lights, the remains of a couple of metal buildings, one of them still topped by an orange wind sock.

Rain came in fits and starts, large drops that popped when they hit the windshield. Alex clicked on the radio and found a station that was playing rock-and-roll. She smiled at me and gave the car a little twist on the road, then laughed and sang along. I watched the road and the horizon. Dzubas came over the back of the seat and rifled the sack for a pear.

Dominica got into town without going through the stretch of burger joints. We came in along the water, then pulled into a gravel and mud lot behind Captain Mike's Oyster Heaven, an old red and blue tugboat propped up on railroad ties, and leaning slightly to one side. The back half of the parking lot was a wire pen.

The door had been cut in the hull and painted to match the lapped siding. The place had a low ceiling, bowed walls, and portholes running along behind the counter. Captain Mike was past fifty, short, with arms as thick as sewer pipes and white hair that bunched behind his ears. He wore khakis and a butcher's apron, and he had a four-day beard. There was only one customer, a guy who looked like a tourist, and he was telling the Captain that the oysters were grainy. With no warning, Captain Mike's oyster knife came across the counter and popped one of the guy's shirt buttons. The customer fell off his stool, sat on the floor for a minute, then got up and rubbed his chest where the knife nicked him. Captain Mike was plopping shell-less oysters on a serving platter, deliberately, making a performance of it. He smiled at the guy. "You like a nice oyster?" he said.

The tourist shook his head, dropped some money on the counter, and went out the way we'd come in. Captain Mike tossed back an oyster, grinned, then leaned across the counter to get his cheek kissed by Dominica. "You been hiding out," he said.

"Family matters," Dominica said, introducing us.

The women got kisses, the rest handshakes. Captain Mike's teeth looked like a collection of tiny football helmets. He waved the knife toward the door. "This boy wouldn't know an oyster if he laid one."

Dominica stepped up on the foot rail to get a lemon from the serving side of the bar, "Still selling 'em sand, huh?"

Captain Mike dragged a golf-ball-size oyster through a pool of red sauce on the counter, then slid the oyster down his tongue. When he'd swallowed he sucked his thumb clean. "I'm gonna sand you little lady, you don't straighten out." He wiped his face on the corner of his apron.

There were only four seats at the bar, so four of us stood up while eating the oysters Captain Mike shucked. He was blindingly fast, opening the shells, freeing the meat, and slipping the half-shell onto the slick counter all in one motion. We had Miller beer in bright, bubble-covered bottles, and did the best we could while he and Dominica carried on their conversation, which was mostly playful insults and threats. He said he thought she ought to have children. She wondered if he wanted to be the father. He wondered if she'd like to have powdered soap on her oysters. She thought there was powdered soap on the oysters.

"With hips like that you'll have it easy," he said, pointing to his own hips. "You ought to see mine."

"I see them," she said. "They're large and old."

"I mean my kid," he said. "She's visiting. Most times her mother keeps her in the country, but she's staying with me a few days now."

"Where?" Dominica said, twisting on her stool to look around the room. "I didn't know you had a daughter."

"She was in the car here a minute ago." He put his face against the glass over the sink. "Probably gone on back to look at the hogs, she loves them hogs." He came out from behind the counter. "I'll show you. Gotta get her outta there anyway."

Three of us followed him outside. At the gate to the pen he passed out galoshes from a heap in a wooden bin. The pen was four inches of mud and a dozen small, football-size pigs white as suet where they weren't spattered with the mud. A bird on stilt-like legs squirted out of our path, then went on poking its head in the slush, looking for something to eat. There was a tree in the center of the pen, and, farther back, two low shacks, each about five feet high. Near the far pen stood a child in a white dress with a bow at the waist, a little girl all dressed up, wearing knee-high rubber boots like ours. She didn't see us. She was standing there in the twilight staring at the wall of the shed.

Captain Mike yelled at her. "What are you doing there? I told you to stay in the car. It's raining out here. Now you come over here, quick now."

For a second the little girl didn't make a move, then she pointed at the shed in front of her and said, "Look, Daddy. See? Isn't it pretty? Come see."

Captain Mike sighed, then started for her, his feet peppering all four of us with mud, scattering the animals, which squeaked as they jumped out of his path. The bird waddled casually after him.

Dominica got between Mel and me and linked arms with both of us, pulling us forward. "Can't stop now," she said.

The second shed was built up against an oak tree. The child was pointing at a groove between two boards in the wet siding where a tiny rainbow shined. Captain Mike picked up the girl and carried her under the shed, ducking to avoid a two-by-six nailed into the tree. Mel and Dominica followed him, and I stayed out, looking at the rainbow. Through the boards I could see them moving around in the shed. Then something caught my eye in one of the cracks—the child, peering out at me. I heard the Captain ask Dominica what my name was, then he yelled, "Say, Martin, you want to carry her on inside for me? We need to have a little talk here."

"Sure," I said, crouching to get into the shed. Dominica and Mel and Captain Mike were sitting on a pew-like seat at the back of the shed. Next to them a huge, purple pig was flopped in a puddle. The pig looked at me. The child was by the door. "Hi," I said to her. "You ready to go?"

She grinned and nodded, so I picked her up, putting a hand on her head to protect her from the two-by. When we got out of the pen I put her on the ground and took off her galoshes. She had black patent leather shoes on. "My name's Magic," she said. "What's yours?"

I told her, and then she took my hand and we started for the tugboat, but stopped by the door while she pointed out a light on a pole. "It looks like a flower," she said. "A blue flower. I know my colors."

Inside I got a rag and wiped off her shoes. Jane cleaned her hands and cheeks. She had beautiful golden brown hair that went down her back to her legs. She told everybody her name was Magic, and she asked their names, repeating each one carefully.

Alex said, "You're pretty, did you know that?"

"Yes," the child said. "Can you play a piano? Do you like the way a piano sounds? I always play mostly on the high notes. Once I was sick and I went to this place where there was a piano, and I played it. Did you ever see an animal licking a tree? Like on a beach somewhere?"

Alex raised an eyebrow at us, then said, "Yes, yes, no, and no, if I got it right. Who calls you Magic?"

"My daddy. He always calls me things, but this time it's Magic. I like it, don't you? Do you know what magic is? It's like camels. There's a camel at this place we go sometimes. It's real big, about seven feet."

"That's a true thing about camels," Turner said. "But what about pancakes? I have a pancake restaurant, like your father's."

"My father hates pancakes," she said.

"You know," Minnie said, "I could show you a horse. Big horse." He spread his arms as wide as he could. "You can ride him forever."

"That's nothing," she said. "Once a horse I know came up and pushed me with his face. I was little then. His face was as big as me."

Alex lifted the girl onto a clean spot on the counter. "Where are our friends?" she said.

"They're meeting out there," I said. "I don't know what they're doing."

"Probably making baby plans," Jane said.

"Multiple babies," Dzubas said. He went to the door and looked out toward the pen. A wet breeze sifted into the room.

"Not cute," Jane said, slapping his shoulder.

"I had a baby once, but she died," the child said. "She got stuck in a combine. I was sad, but I guess it didn't matter because she wasn't a real baby. Do you think camels are as furry as they look on TV? My camel doesn't have any fur at all. It's green. They aren't really green, are they?"

"Not often," Alex said. "Furry, but never green."

"I've only seen them in black and white, so I didn't know."

"Maybe on radio?" Turner said.

"Radio, radio, all the livelong day," Dzubas said. "Should somebody go out there and see if everything's all right?"

"I'll go," Alex said.

She didn't have to. Dominica came in, letting the screen door slam behind her. She washed her hands in the sink behind the counter, then took the child off the bar and said, "We're taking a walk, O. K.?" She grinned at Alex. "Mel will be here in a minute. Then we'll go back."

Dzubas grabbed Jane's hand. "We're going for a walk too," he said, turning to her. "O. K.?"

"What's everybody going for walks all of the sudden?" Turner said. "It's raining out here, isn't it?" He followed Dzubas to the door.

"Sprinkling," Jane said, as she went out.

I went to the cooler and asked Minnie and Turner if they wanted beer. They didn't.

I got one and drank it, studying the decorations in the room—framed clippings, autographed photos of people I didn't know, store-bought oil paintings, ropes, harpoons and gaffs. Behind the bar there were postcards pinned to the wall, and there was an ERA article from *Time*.

Minnie said, "Pretty little girl, isn't she?"

"She's up on the pancake problem," Turner said.

"Talks a lot," I said.

"Yep," Minnie said.


WE DROVE FAST going back to SeaSide. Ours were the only cars on the highway. The rain was flying sideways in the beams of our headlights and in the glow of Dominica's taillights. It was chilly in the car. I would rather have been with Dominica, alone on a ride like this, on a dark night, returning from Odalisque through winter rain, windows sealed and quiet, dash lights sparkling. I was pleased that people were leaving. I even allowed myself to think about moving to Florida, about living at SeaSide. I thought about Alex, and about how I had spent the last years of our marriage assuring myself of the limits of my curiosity about other women, explaining my stares, my infatuations with skin, soft hair, glittering makeup, skirts whipped by a long stride, with pale shoulders, open blouses, lips, eyes and thighs and ankles of women in the streets, with tight rumps and with the small reliefs of welted Levi seams, with icy glances, eyeliner, belts, and flesh-colored sandals, explaining the desire I found and felt in a voice, the twist of a mouth, a particular turn of the head, a casual hand brushing my cheek. I convinced myself that it was innocent, to be expected, but I could not convince Alex. Now I knew she was right. The divorce was right. I turned around in the front seat and looked at her. She was staring straight through the rain, through the wipers beating the rain away. Orange and green reflections from the dashboard streaked her face. She looked paralyzed—hands on the bottom of the wheel, one knee cocked, back straight, eyes forward. I wondered, as I had often wondered when we were together, what she was thinking of, what she was planning, hoping. If I asked she wouldn't say, she'd tell me that she had been thinking of nothing, or that she could not remember, or that she was thinking about the way the rain looked as it bounced away from the windshield. Then she would give me a fierce look and tell me that she did not like to be interrogated.

So I didn't ask. I leaned my head against the window in my door, stared at the blurred road slipping by outside, felt my forehead bump against the cold glass. When the blur became unsettling I quit looking.

The party scattered quickly once we got home. By midnight I was alone in my apartment, sitting in the bed staring at a replay of a college football game on ESPN. Dominica came in so quietly I didn't hear her until she was standing in the bedroom door. She looked tired. She took her shoes off in that handsome way some women have of shedding clothes and formality at the same time, and then she stayed in the door, holding the shoes as if they were hand grenades.

I touched the bedspread and said, "Want to sit?"

"I can't stay," she said. "Not tonight."

I nodded. "O. K. That's fine." I slid my legs off the bed. "For the moment you're just standing there looking slim and elegant? Slightly tortured?"

"Slightly," she said, smiling. She came and sat next to me on the side of the bed. "Everybody's leaving tomorrow. It feels funny. Usually I'm so glad when people leave."

"It'll be fine," I said, crossing my feet. "Alex is going too?"

"She has a noon flight at Fort Myers. I asked her to wait a couple of days, but she said she had to go. You don't have any brothers and sisters, do you?"

"Nope. I was glad about it when I was a kid, but I'm not now. Maybe I wasn't glad about it, I just think I was."

"Nothing to be glad about," she said. "I'd have died if Alex wasn't around. My friends were on the distant side, even the best ones. Sometimes I think family is all that counts. You live or die with them. Spouses never quite make it, you know what I mean? They make it for the kids, but not for each other. It's close . . . I guess it's a different kind of thing." She and I went into the bathroom. She didn't close the door. "Don't listen," she said. "Why don't you get us a drink."

I started for the other room. "Drink drink? Coke?"

"Tab," she said. "Please."

I had to go out in the atrium to the machine to get the drinks. When I got back she was standing at the bedroom window. I gave her a can and looked out at the Gulf. There was an odd silver light in the sky, like a lozenge-shaped patch against the darker gray around it. She said, "You ought to go back with her, with Alex."

"I wasn't invited," I said. "It's too late anyway. In a week or so we're single again."

"You looked invited to me," she said. She took a drink of her Tab and then settled into one of the plastic-tube chairs.

I squinted at her. "What's that, jealousy? What a great idea."

She smiled. "Maybe a little. It's a jungle out here in girl-land. We're like these pathetically dumb animals, and we lose it now and then. You guys are worse, of course. Alex has such great eyes. She looks at you and you know you've been looked at."

"I guess," I said. "I don't remember what color they are."

"It ain't the color I'm talking about," Dominica said.

"That's a good thing," I said. "If you were talking about the color I wouldn't know what you were talking about."

"Blue, motherfucker," she said.

I laughed. "Yes, ma'am. I remember now. I'm seeing a blue aspect, around the eyes and the eye-area."

"That isn't it, anyway. You ought to stay together if you can. It's better than going around hunting for somebody you don't hate on sight."

"Wait a minute. I want to look this up in the program. Where does it say the girl exhibits low-grade depression?" I sat on the arm of her chair, but the chair bent precariously, so I got off. I said, "I've got it. Let's . . . take a pill. Or . . . exercise, bathe till our skin boils, sleep like rocks."

"I'd like to sleep like a rock," she said. "Maybe thirty years."

"Uh-huh," I said. "Why don't we do tonight for starters? Work up to the big one." I took her hand and pulled her out of the chair. "It could be the chair. When I sit there I start feeling kind of poorly. Even when I look over to that side of the room I don't feel so good—maybe we ought to burn it. Get in on the noxious fumes craze."

She leaned against me as if she were about to fall. "Ready when you are," she said. "Pass the nozzle."

WE HAD an early breakfast at the Pancake House. Turner took our orders without comment or suggestion, Mel played with two magnets he'd bought at the Mini-Mart, chasing one across the table with the other, Minnie talked about the drive they were preparing for, Jane and Dzubas bickered about the toast, Dominica didn't look any worse than she had the night before, and Alex went through the entire meal without taking her hand off my leg. I hadn't slept well. Walking Dominica back to her apartment, we had run into Alex sitting by the pool, and Dominica had decided to stay there with her for a time. I felt awkward, so I had gone back to my place.

After the meal we drove back to SeaSide and stood in the parking lot while Minnie and Mel loaded the motorcycle into the bed of the pickup.

"It's a great day, isn't it?" Minnie said, when they'd gotten the bike secured. "I'm a morning person, I think. I love this light—it's so thin. Know what I mean, thin? It's almost like this light is practicing for later on. A bunch of the rays haven't showed up yet. It's really great."

Mel was wearing dark glasses. "It makes me sick to my stomach," he said.

Dominica had an arm around his waist. "You hate what everybody else likes," she said. "That's always the way you were. It's constitutional."

"Historical embeddedness," he said. He shook my hand and then kissed Alex, who had her arm looped through mine. He stepped back and studied us, cocking his head back and forth. "Look here," he said to Dominica, pointing at us. "A little silver man in the mirror with the girl of his dreams—that painting we saw in Philadelphia, remember?"

She looked. "Don't remember. Was that the time you wouldn't sleep with me in the hotel because I wore a white dress without a slip and you said I looked like a K Mart checker?"

"I never said that. I promise." Mel looked at the sky and clapped his hands together as if in prayer. "And if I did, I repudiate it."

"I always liked K Mart checkers," Dzubas said. "They're so sexy in those trash outfits. They remind me of gas station bathrooms."

Jane said, "Our disgusting companion, Puke Blipskin. Say a few words for the folks, will you, Puke?" She held her fist in Dzubas's face.

"They smell sexy. I can't help it," he said. "Pardon me for visiting your planet."

Jane made a retching gesture, twisting her face to one side and poking her finger into her mouth.

"Must be all that old urine," Alex said. "I can swing with that." She laughed, and Dominica laughed, and Mel smiled, and Minnie looked across the road at the Gulf.

Jane said, "Lord, would you please forgive all these people for this? They are trying to say good-bye to these two over here"—she pointed at Mel and Minnie—"and they aren't doing a real good job of it, but if you can hang in, I am confident that they will get it done. O. K.?"

"Thanks, Jane," Mel said. He started to shake her hand, but she got up on her toes and kissed him. Then he hugged Dominica, signaled the rest of us, and got into the truck.

Dominica took Minnie's hand and led him to the driver's side. "I love the horse," she said.

He looked at Dominica as if he were the one who ought to have been married to her. "Me too," he said, wiping his mouth and chin on his shoulder. "I got you a surprise, too. In my room. I hope you like it."

She smiled and pulled his hand to her face, kissing the back of his wrist, then putting the wrist to her cheek. "I'm crazy about it, and I don't even know what it is." She gave him a push.

"My rhino," he said. "I blew him up for you. It was real hard. He almost gave me a hernia, but I kept blowing and blowing, know what I mean?"

Dominica did a lovely silent-movie laugh.


FOUR GUYS in white jackets were at work setting up the atrium for the local garden club luncheon. Two of them worked the round wooden tables and folding chairs, and the other two were setting up a buffet. Together, they made a considerable racket. Dominica said she had to be available, so she went to her apartment. I went to sit with Alex while she packed.

When we got into the room Alex switched on the Weather Channel. The guy who was talking about the weather did most of his presentation standing right in front of Florida. He was worried about the Gulf Coast, and spent a lot of time pointing to coastal states, which were covered with rain dashes. Below that there was another patch of rain with sinister-looking black arrows pok-

ing out of it. "Cold front," Alex said, standing in front of
the TV.

"We look pretty clear," I said.

"Who can see us?" she said. "Besides, it's closing in. I
smelled it when we were outside. I hate flying in storms."

"You could stick around," I said.

"No. I couldn't. You have to go back, too, don't you?
Or are you on permanent leave?"

"I have to do something." I got a can of Tab out of the
refrigerator, then sat on the couch watching the radar circle the television screen.

She went into the bedroom and brought out her suitcase, which she opened on the couch beside me. "I don't
have much to pack," she said. "Oh, I wanted to tell you
something." She stopped rearranging the clothes in the
suitcase and grinned at me. "You know the manager in
the grocery store at home? The one you always said I
wanted to sleep with? Well, you were right."

"C'mon, Alex," I said. I closed my eyes and ran a hand
through my hair. "Why are you telling me this?"

"Who else am I going to tell?" Alex said. "I told Dominica and she said I was a sleazoid. I mean, you were
gone. I got sexed up and went over there one day, and
that was it. Like in the movies. It was quick. We went
home and screwed." She started back into the bedroom,
but stopped by the door and said, "I was surprised how
easy it was."

When she turned away again I threw the can of Tab at
her. It hit her on the butt and bounced up onto the dining table, spinning and spewing the drink all over the
place.

She yelled when the can hit her, but then cut it off and stood there rubbing her backside. She didn't look at me. In a minute she went through the door into the bedroom, then came out with a towel that she tossed at me. "Clean it," she said.

I shot her the finger. "Clean this, sweetie."

She shot me the finger.

We remained like that, her in the bedroom door, me on the couch, shooting each other the finger, for a few seconds. Both of us put on the ugliest smiles we could manage. It didn't last long. She quit first, sighed, went into the bedroom for more clothes. I got the towel and started on the table. We didn't say anything else.

She made two more trips into the bedroom, and I finished with the table top and wiped off the wall. When she was done packing she went into the kitchen and came out with a half-used roll of paper towels, and both of us got down on the floor trying to sponge the Tab out of the carpet.

"I guess it wasn't what I wanted to hear," I said.

"I guess not," she said.

"I'm sorry."

She sat up on her heels and refolded the towels she'd been using on the carpet. "Me too," she said, looking at her hands. She sat that way for a moment, playing with the paper, then laughed a little.

"What?" I said.

"I was thinking about when you threw the typewriter into the wall, remember? The hole? I was terrified. I thought you might kill me."

I kept leaning on my lump of paper towels.

She got up and rubbed her backside some more. "That really hurt," she said. "You could have hit me in the face."

"You were turned the other way," I said. "I waited for that."

"You waited so I wouldn't see it coming," she said. "Anyway, you could have hit my head. That would have been a real experience—high drama. Ambulances. Flashing lights. Criminal prosecution. TV Movie of the Week."

"Not what we were trained for," I said.

She slumped into the couch. "I know. It's the same with the stupid grocery guy. I wanted to try it, know what I mean? But he got there and he was wrong. I mean, in the house. Like he was a plumber, or something. I don't mean his plumber-ness was the problem, but . . . oh, you know what I mean."

I looked at the remaining spots on the carpet. "I thought that's what you were after."

"Maybe. Until he arrived." She closed her suitcase and slid her palm over its top several times. "He was O. K. I mean, I'm not afraid of him. I've been back to his store. That's kind of . . . something."

I picked up some soggy towels and tossed them from hand to hand.

"Oops. Sorry," she said.

"What if we change the subject?" I said, getting off the floor. I took the paper towels into the kitchen. Then I took the bath towel into the bathroom.

When I got back, Alex was crouched by the television. "I wish this guy wouldn't stand in front of Florida all the time. How are people down here supposed to know any-thing? I hate the way they do this—there, see that?" She pointed to the left edge of the screen, and said, in a child-like voice, "We're really looking over here to the side, but we're pretending we're looking at this map, which isn't there, and everybody knows it . . . Hey! Bozo!" She hit a knuckle on the screen. "You don't fool me. You're wav-ing at a wall there, Bozo."

She clicked off the set and watched the picture disap-pear, then got to her feet and started inspecting the table and the floor.

"Look O. K.?" I said.

"Like new," she said. "No one will ever know what went on here today. These stains look like the other stains. Good work." She patted my shoulder, then took the suitcase and put it by the door. "I've got to go," she said.

"I'll get the bag," I said.

"You do that," she said. "I'm ducking in here a min-ute. I'll meet you outside." She slipped past me into the bedroom.

I took her suitcase and went out into the atrium. The caterers had all the tables up and covered with clean white tablecloths. The pool was empty and absolutely calm. The sun coming in the east windows made a sharp shadow line on the building, across the AstroTurf, and up and down among the tables. The space seemed bigger and more forlorn and dusty than it had since I came. A couple of women in pale, floral dresses were already sit-ting at one of the tables. The caterers in their white coats were standing by the buffet, smoking and talking.

I waited by the pool. I was looking at the water, wondering why it didn't seem as odd and pretty as it was, and thinking about how you couldn't separate the color from the thing itself, when Dzubas yelled, "Don't do it! Things aren't what they seem." He was in the door to his apartment, holding a telephone.

"Are you sure?" I cocked my head and held a hand above my eyes so I could see him against the sunlight.

He shrugged. "No. Not really. But, think of it this way—you go in and you have to come right back out again. Sounds dreary to me."

"Thanks," I said.

"Don't mention it," he said. He held up the phone. "I'm waiting for a call to tell me I bought the bush on plywood."

Alex had come out of the apartment. She put a hand on my shoulder and said, "Keep an eye on my boy, here, will you?"

Dzubas nodded and crossed one leg over the other, leaning against his doorframe.

I got the suitcase and we went around the end of the pool away from the garden club setup. Dominica's door was open, so we went in. She was at her desk in the tiny dining area next to the kitchen. "Ready?" she said.

"Yep. We are ready," Alex said, hugging her sister. "It's nice seeing you."

Dominica said, "Me too. But we'll see each other soon, won't we?"

"I hope so," Alex said.

I followed them to the parking lot, said good-bye, shaking Alex's hand and kissing her on the cheek, then

watched as the two of them embraced. When they separated Dominica was crying. We stood together as Alex
drove off, and then I started to hug Dominica, but she
spun away and said I should be the one crying.

"I did," I said. "Hours on end. But I don't feel so bad
now."

"Well I feel hollow inside, and I don't want to talk
about it, either, not now. I want to sit in my room." She
made a move as if to touch my arm, but didn't touch me,
and started for the front door of the building.

I said, "I'm going across the street. I'll check in later."

"Fine," she said, lifting a hand over her shoulder.

I walked along the water for a few minutes, but it was
hard to walk in the sand, and I hadn't wanted to go to the
beach in the first place, so I crossed the street again, fig-
uring that I'd go to my room and wait until lunch. The
speaker at the garden club luncheon, a young man with
smooth long hair and a clerical collar, was finishing his
talk when I got inside. I went up the stairs listening to
him. "Let me ask you to imagine a decaying urban neigh-
borhood," he said. "And at the center of this neighbor-
hood there is a garden." He made a grand gesture with
his arm. "A luxurious garden in a meadow rich with
lovely flowers. Can you see it? There is a stone path, and
there are scattered petals on the stones, and the path is
edged with thick grasses, and this winding path comes to
a bridge over a brook, and the brook is of clear water
rushing over smooth rocks. By the side of the brook tall
willows stand, their leaves drooping to touch the water.
Beyond the bridge, which is of intricately carved and
painted wood, the path rises slightly, twisting back along

the bank toward a pagoda that stands off in a group of swaying rain trees, and in the pagoda the water can still be heard. Now imagine, if you will, that two young men enter the garden. The first sits on the steps of the pagoda and reflects on the hissing breeze, the rippling leaves, the quiet reports of footsteps on the path, and he is sad, for he realizes that the garden is only a garden in the center of a large and wretched city, that the meadow turns into a dump a few hundred yards away, that the brook narrows and becomes an open sewer, that the rustling trees give way to rusting wrecked cars, that the grassy knolls becomes heaps of half-eaten garbage circled by green-winged flies the size of thumbs. The second young man, almost the twin of the first, walks the path, stands on the bridge, wades in the shallow, clear brook, rests in the high, lush grass of the bank, and he is not sad at all, but charmed to be in the garden, because the garden is so beautiful." The speaker stopped to admonish the crowd with a stiffly pointed finger. He took a drink from a clear plastic tumbler. He waited at the makeshift podium for the murmurs among the garden club women to die down, and then he concluded, "The point of this story? It is that the first young man's sadness is genuine and accurate, his perception unarguable, his view moderate, what we might call reasoned. The second young man, the one whose sight and thought do not stray from the garden, who is charmed, however narrowly, is a superficial creature, a clown. But remember this: when the first young man leaves the garden, he is only right. When the second leaves, he is happy."

There wasn't much applause, and then there was more,

as if the ladies were suddenly embarrassed for the speaker. Then the pace of the applause quickened, and the noise echoed in the atrium, filling it with a sound like cards on spoked bicycle wheels, and the ladies downstairs were smiling and nodding as they applauded, and the speaker stood his ground and waved, smiling and nodding as they were. After a minute I pushed off the railing and started to go into my apartment, clapping as hard as I could.

I SPENT the afternoon waiting for Dominica. I called her apartment twice, but she didn't answer. Finally, I decided it was silly to sit a couple of rooms from each other, so I went down to her apartment and knocked on the door. She opened it wearing a white t-shirt that said UNAFFECT-ING BLUR in small black type across the chest. She looked sleepy. This was about six o'clock. She held the door open about ten inches and didn't invite me in. I said, "Hi. You want to do something?"

"Like what?" she said. She was hanging back behind the door and squinting at me.

"I don't know," I said. "Take a look at Minnie's rhino? Take a drive? Eat?"

"The rhino's in here, I hate drives, and I'm not hungry."

"Right," I said. I turned and looked at the empty pool. "Swim?"

"I hate to swim," she said. She was still behind the door. It was dark in her apartment. "I don't think I'm going to do anything."

"Invite me in? Sit on the couch? Watch TV?"

She stroked her head as if she were pushing her hair out of the way. "I don't think so. I'll be all right tomorrow. I want to rest."

"I know what you mean," I said. "It's strange when all these people leave all of a sudden."

"That's not what I mean," she said.

I shook my head. "Me either." I was standing there trying to think of the next thing to say when Jane walked up with a galvanized steel bucket half full of sand.

"Take a look at this," she said. "I got all this off my floor. Can you believe it?" She showed me the bucket. "Hey, Dominica. What are you doing, hiding in there?" She looked from one of us to the other. "Are you guys having a famous final scene? I'd better get out, huh?"

"What did you use?" Dominica said, stepping around the door so she could see into the bucket.

"Broom," Jane said. "Two hours' worth. Actually, some of it's from Dzubas's. His place is worse than mine."

"You could have borrowed the big vacuum," Dominica said. "You know where it is, don't you?"

Jane pointed across the pool toward the supply room.

Dominica nodded. "Just get it when you want it. Really."

Jane backed up and started to leave, holding the bucket in front of her with two hands on the handle. "I go for brooms. They make me feel like I'm doing something."

Dominica was all the way out from behind the door, standing on one foot, the toes of her other foot curled on the top of the first. When Jane was gone, Dominica looked at me and said, "Well, we can't stand out here." It was dark inside except for the drapes, which were glowing over the windows. She turned on a ceramic table lamp that was a rabbit with a shade on its head, and sat on the couch. "As long as we don't have to go for a walk. Please, God."

I said, "O. K. What's going on? Why so glum? Is all this about Alex?"

"What I should do is be direct, right?" She pulled the tail of the t-shirt down. "Well, I'm leaving. I'm going to stay with her for a while. I don't know, maybe we won't get along. But I'm trying it. I've already called Isabel. She's going to come over here and watch out for things. Not all the time. A couple times a week. I'm just hanging on here. The whole place is hanging on. So maybe I'll get a job over there, something like that. Join the rest of the folks."

I said, "So. That's the news?"

She smiled, but it wasn't the smile I wanted to see. I knew the rest. I didn't want to sit there and have her tell me about it, but I couldn't get up and walk out. We stared at each other for a long time. At first I was trying to get my bearings, but the staring went on too long and I started thinking about how silly I must have looked. I wanted to say something to break things up, but I wasn't mad, and I didn't want to make those nervous jokes people make. At the same time, giving her the blank stare was the movie version of the scene, and I didn't want to do that either. I wasn't doing a great job. She looked relieved. Her skin was unbearably smooth and taut, her eyes clear. I tried to straighten up and suddenly I felt huge, like a giant. The rabbit lamp shimmered and the glowing drapes made me want to cry. Dominica seemed frail and determined—she was sitting there with me so she could transfer this information about our future, about the absence of it. She was being patient. I could feel her patience. She was waiting for me to get it.

I said, "Are you sure?"

She stepped over the coffee table and sat on the arm of my chair. She relaxed and reached to brush the hair from my temple, but stopped short. "You don't want to be touched," she said.

"It's O. K.," I said. But when she reached out again, I caught her wrist and pulled her into my lap.

"Please," she said, trying to free herself.

"Take it easy," I said. "Quit it."

"Don't do this," she said. She got one hand free and twisted herself so she could push against my chest. Her face had changed again. She looked frightened.

My arms were locked around her waist. She couldn't get off my lap. I opened my legs and one of hers slipped down between them. I said, "Dominica. Please. Settle down a minute."

"Let me go," she said. She ripped at my hands, scraping with her nails, bending my fingers. When that didn't work she slugged my hands a couple times with her fist. "You jerk," she said. "What the fuck are you doing? This isn't funny."

I held her waist with one arm, and with my other hand grabbed her breast. I squeezed it, and I wiggled it back and forth, and I said, "This little piggy went to market . . ."

She pulled loose and fell on the floor, then got up and

looked for something to hit me with. I didn't move. I
slouched in the chair with a hand on my forehead, looking at my lap.

She said, "Get out."

I said, "I'm sorry." I wasn't looking at her, I was sitting
there shaking my head. Finally I looked up and slowly
said, "Don't worry about it. Please." I made a noisy sigh
through my nose and got out of the chair. She picked up
the rabbit lamp. I held up my hands. "Really. I'm done.
I'm leaving," I said, backing out of the room, hands up all
the way. She stayed where she was. I checked the door to
be sure it would lock behind me as I went out.

The atrium was empty and the water in the pool was
still, reflecting the ceiling lights. I looked for a minute,
then thought I'd go outside. I sat on one of the chairs out
there, scanning the landscape, taking in the peculiar blu-
ish light. The horse on the beach seemed as if it was leaning to one side. I started to go across the street and take a
look, but I lost interest as soon as I hit the beach, so I
came back and walked around the abandoned Tastee
Freeze. There were lots of bugs inside the building. From
the parking lot I could see in through the glass end of the
SeaSide atrium. A couple of people were walking around
inside, and that reminded me of sitting in the parking lot
at the mall near our house, waiting for Alex to finish
shopping. I always liked parking lots, especially big ones
at dusk, or at night, the way they look, all that open
space, the glass in the cars shining, reflecting the lights;
different kinds of lots, landscaped ones with cars on different levels, slopes painted with bright directions, boxed
trees plump and squat, and wide open ones that stretch

hundreds of yards in every direction, punctuated with store signs in harsh colors and careful letters, or curious, circus-like letters that sizzle against dark buildings, or ink-blue sky; and they're wonderful when it rains, or when it has rained, they're even better then than usual because of the way the light splinters and glitters all over the place, and because of how things sound, how it sounds on a cool night when a car rolls through a puddle nearby, or when two or three shoppers walk past, talking, their voices distinct but not quite decipherable, or when there's a breeze going in fits across the blacktop, blowing paper cups in manic half-circles, dragging crumpled cardboard boxes, rolling a soft drink bottle. And the look of dark shapes coming out of the buildings, coats flapping, hair blown, noisy packages at their sides. Or when the lots are almost empty, very late at night, when most of the stores are closed and a few cars dot this flat place with its hundred painted spines, and the cars are in groups, a few here under the light, two by the drugstore entrance, a line of a half-dozen there at the edge of the lot. And when it's cold and the motor's running, and some driver obviously waiting on someone drives slowly through the lot, his path a nonsense of backtracks, circles, weavings through the parked cars, his exhaust powdering the air as he goes.

I walked for another ten minutes, and then I went inside and called Delta and got on a ten o'clock flight to Tampa. Then I called Dzubas and asked if he could give me a ride into Fort Myers.

"Now?" he said.

I said now. We agreed to meet at the car at nine. At eight-thirty I was ready, so I sat in the room with the windows open and watched the white lines in the surf for half an hour. The weather had come up again. A thunderstorm was rolling in off the Gulf. There was lightning far off, out over the water. The moon was shifting in and out of dirty gray clouds. There was a good breeze.

Everybody was standing by the Mercedes when I got down there. I couldn't figure out who was driving me, or if all of them were going along. Nobody was very happy.

The trunk was open. I dropped my suitcase in there and shut the lid. Jane was the first one to say good-bye. She gave me a hug. She was small. I felt her belt buckle against my leg.

Turner handed me a plastic bag with one of his "beef in a blanket" pancakes inside. "Throw it out the window if you don't want it," he said. "Something'll eat it."

I thanked him and shook his hand, but I was watching Dominica, who was getting into the car. He looked at her too. "Thought we had it," he said.

Dzubas grabbed my hand. "Take it slow," he said.

I nodded. The three of them walked with me, giving the car a wide berth, making small talk, staring off this way and that. Dzubas held the corner of my door as I got in. Dominica said, "I'm driving you if that's O. K. I want to."

I said it was fine.

There were a few rain spots on the windshield, but they vanished as soon as we got on the highway. For a few miles she didn't say anything and I didn't either. We watched the road slide under us. After a while I managed to get out another awkward apology for grabbing her the way I had, and she accepted the apology, saying it didn't matter much anyway, although it was a messy way to do things.

"I wasn't myself," I said.

"Who were you, some kind of hockey king? I couldn't believe you were doing that."

"Won't happen again," I said.

"I didn't expect you to leave like this," she said.

"That's what I figured," I said, tapping my knuckle on the glass on my side of the car.

"You could have stayed another couple of days. We could've gone together, flown over there."

"Yeah. That'd be fun."

"O. K.," she said. "Sorry. It isn't what I meant, anyway. I meant we could have spent a little more time together."

"Why don't you just pull over? We can spend time together right here."

She let out a sigh and turned to look at me. "You don't have to be ugly. I'm not thrilled. I'm not winning."

We drove through a shower that started without warning, went on for a quarter mile, and then turned sprinkly. I rolled down the window to let the wind blow some rain in on me. Finally, I said, "You're planning to go in a couple days?"

"I think so," she said. "There really isn't much to do, and I want to see what it's like there. I mean, I may come back in a week."

"Maybe I should hang around," I said, trying to make it sound playful.

"Maybe I'll call you," she said.

After that we seemed out of things to say, so I spent

the rest of the drive staring out in front of the car, watching stripes zip by, looking at billboards, counting miles on
state signs. When we got to the outskirts of Fort Myers
we passed a mall and I saw a clock on a bank that said it
was nine-fifty. I said, "We'd better hurry or you're going
to have me for another couple of days."

"That's an idea," she said.

The airport looked like two dusty nineteen-forties gas
stations slammed together and converted for the new
purpose. They hadn't spent a lot of time on the job, just
closed in the bays with walls of square windows, polished
up the floor, and put a few too-healthy plants in eye-
catching spots. We went across the empty waiting room,
then waited while the uniformed guard, a wormy guy who
looked as if he'd had the job for fifty years, searched my
suitcase on a folding table. He had a cobra patch on his
sleeve at the shoulder of his shirt, and what looked like
insects tattooed on the back of his left hand. He went
through the suitcase much more thoroughly than he
needed to. I watched him carefully, and when he shut the
case I smiled at him. He didn't like that. I started to turn
and say good-bye to Dominica, but she wasn't there. I
scanned the lobby trying to find her. She was gone. The
guard said, "You got a problem, Bub?" I asked him what
happened to the woman I was with, and he shook his
head and pointed to the metal detector. I went through it
backwards, still searching the room. The snack shop was
closed, the rental car booth had its lights on but there
wasn't anybody inside. There was a young guy at the ticket
counter working over some old stubs or something. That
was it. She wasn't in the building. The guard finished fid-

dling with his meter and told me to go through the detector again, so I did that, and then he dropped my bag to
the floor and slid it to me with his foot. I took a last look
around and then went out the door he pointed at. The
plane was old and small, and only a hundred feet from
the terminal. The pilot's compartment had a blue curtain
where the door was supposed to be, and that was open, so
when I took a seat I could look up the aisle and see the
instruments glowing in the dark. He was drinking coffee
out of a styrofoam cup and laughing with the flight attendant, who was about half in his lap. She didn't notice me
come in. There were three other passengers, Navy kids
who looked sleepy, in the back of the plane. The main interior lights were off, so the cabin was lit by a half-dozen
reading bulbs that were dropping fans of stale-looking
light on as many seats. I clicked mine off. In a couple of
minutes a guy with two red-tipped flashlights, one in each
pocket, ran up the stairs, said something to the pilot, then
clanked down again, and rolled the boarding ramp out of
the way. The woman came out of the front compartment
and locked the ramp hatch, then walked past me, smiling,
checking my seat belt. The pilot stuffed his cup in a plastic bag hanging on the console between his seat and the
co-pilot's, then started flipping switches. The engine on
the far side of the fuselage rumbled and caught. The
lights dimmed and the plane started vibrating. I leaned
against the scratched plastic window and looked out at a
fruit drink machine with a cartoon of a dancing girl on its
display panel. My propeller began to go.

Printed in the United States
by Baker & Taylor Publisher Services